The Wrong Side of the Law

A Tragedy in Five Acts

*

Norman Deeley

Carn Publishing

To my Father

First Published in Great Britain 2005

ISBN 0-9518128-3-1

Published by
Carn Publishing
Lochnoran House
Auchinleck
Ayrshire
KA18 3JW

Printed by Walker & Connell, Ltd.
Hastings Square
Darvel
Ayrshire
KA17 0DS

Contents

ACT ONE

SCENE 1

[February 1902, Glasgow. The office of George Watson, Headmaster of Strathbungo School. The lights come up on Watson, a grave yet humane man of middle years. He is seated behind his desk with a chair in front and is formally dressed in the manner of the time. He is re-reading a report, the seriousness of which is reflected in his face. There is a knock at the door.]

WATSON: *[With authority.]* Come in!

[John Maclean enters. He is a young man in his early twenties, neatly dressed in a three-piece suit, clean-shaven with his hair tidily in place. He has a determined air of quiet conviction about him. Maclean speaks with few gestures, using his hands only occasionally to make a point.]

MACLEAN: You wanted to see me, Sir?

WATSON: Yes, Maclean, come in and sit down. *[He indicates the chair with a nod. While Maclean crosses the room and sits, Watson looks at him severely and glances back to the report.]* Now, Maclean, I suppose you are aware of why I have summoned you here. I am going to give you some advice, advice which it will pay you well to heed. From this time on, you will do exactly what I tell you to in this school!

MACLEAN: *[Quietly but firmly.]* With respect, Sir, I don't think or feel I have done anything amiss.

WATSON: Amiss? Amiss? I've had two parents up here already this morning and both of them have been complaining about you. And you know fine well that parents don't ever come to schools! Another parent has written to the authorities saying you should be removed forthwith and the Inspector from Govan School Board has been at me wanting to know what's been going on. Now I've been fair to you and I've given you every chance but if you won't help yourself there's nothing more *I* can do for you! *[Pauses.]* And you sit there pretending there's nothing wrong!

MACLEAN: I think I know what you are referring to, Sir. This business of religious education. Well, you know my views on the matter. There is no God, and I refuse to teach the children of Glasgow things I do not believe in and things I know to be palpably false.

WATSON: *[Becoming angry.]* Listen, and listen hard, Maclean. You have been teaching barely a couple of years now. I've been at this game a lot longer than you and I'm telling you that there's a God in *this* school and that's what you will tell the children and that's all there is about it! God is on the curriculum and you will instruct the pupils in the rudiments of Christianity and The Bible and you will do that otherwise you will be seen to have failed in your duty!

MACLEAN: *[Becoming angry too.]* With respect, Mr Watson, I *won't* be doing it. I was brought up in the Secession Church and I went to the Free Church Training College and I have listened to it all my waking life and now I am sick of it! What does the Kirk want to know about the poverty of those children sitting in the classrooms? What does the Kirk want to know about bare feet and ragged clothes and unfed bellies? What does the Kirk want to know about the breweries making a fortune out of their parents? What does the Kirk want to know about their housing conditions or their working conditions? Don't ask me to bring them up as Christians! That's the last thing I would wish on anyone.

[From this point on, tempers remain heated.]

WATSON: *[Stands and points.]* You're straying from the issue, Maclean! You were happy to take all the benefits which Christianity gave you and now you don't want others to get the chance. That's selfishness. You are a lucky man you kept your mouth shut about your views until you got your Parchment. If the authorities had known about this beforehand, you would be standing on the street corner in the rain blowing your far-fetched ideas to the wind and not earning a steady salary from teaching. *[Sarcastically.]* And remember in your supercilious pride that you're not the only one in this school who cares about the children. *I'm* responsible for their welfare so don't think for one minute *I* like to see them with lice in their hair. You're not going to change the world by yourself. *[Pauses.]* Now, the point is this. Religious instruction is part of your job and you cannot refuse to do your job. You *will* teach the children what they are legally required to be taught and you will do it without mentioning Plato or Shelley or Marx. The children have to go out as Christians into a Christian world. All the other teachers manage to do it and there is no reason why *you* should not!

MACLEAN: *[Passionately.]* A Christian world! Not for the people in Ireland and Africa and Russia and South America! If there was a God, and if that God was worthy of the praise of the people, then these things would not be happening! Superstition!

WATSON: *[Explosively.]* Superstition! That really is enough, Maclean! I've tried to give you a fair hearing but you'll have to be prepared to defend your case before the ministers on the School Board of Governors. *[Looking away.]* I can't help you any more.

MACLEAN: *[Unflinching.]* I *am* ready. And I'll have a lot more to tell them besides. The interests of the Church are opposed to the interests of the poor. The Highland Clearances proved that once and for all. The people who create the wealth have neither land nor money and that's why I, a Maclean from Mull, am here as a teacher in Glasgow! *[Pauses, then adds in a quieter tone.]* Not to teach religion will not solve all the problems. There are other things to tackle besides.

WATSON: *[Resignedly, as one who has experienced before how the world works.]* Well, they'll probably transfer you to another school and give you one last chance. You'd be a fool not to take it. *[Rises from his chair and walks towards the centre of the room with his back to*

Maclean.] And then there's the matter of the tawse. *[There is an expectant silence.]* I hear you have been encouraging the other teachers not to use corporal punishment on the children. Is this true?

MACLEAN: *[Looks straight ahead.]* Yes.

WATSON: *[Walks back to face Maclean and adds thoughtfully.]* This is another thing which will count against you. The idea is so unrealistic it borders on the insane. People want to see order in their schools and parents want to see their children disciplined. You are paid to educate and that means to keep discipline.

MACLEAN: *[With equal conviction.]* The idea might seem absurd to you but it doesn't to me. I refuse to beat into submission the children of the working class. I refuse to be part of a system which deliberately maintains a huge mass of ignorant, unhealthy people until it needs them for cheap, mobile labour in its factories and its mines or in its wars then dumps them on the rubbish heap when it sees no further use for them. The same system can find resources for its armies and its weapons of mass destruction. And that's what I'll be telling the Christian Governors.

WATSON: *[Sitting on the edge of the table.]* Well, I've been instructed to make out an official report of this meeting and I will be doing so. I've no doubt that the relevant authorities will be in touch. *[A school bell rings in the distance and forces a pause.]* Just remember that the taxes of those you hold in such contempt pay your salary. That will be all just now.

MACLEAN: Sir. *[Exit. Watson sits heavily in his chair as the lights fade on him.]*

***

SCENE II

[April 1904, Greenock. A cold evening outside the gates of a sugar refinery. The wind is blowing directly across the Clyde from the snow-covered Argyll mountains. It is a depressed industrial scene. Light is fading and there is a steady smirr of rain. An upturned box provides a speaker's platform. A group of four refinery workers are waiting around the box, stamping their feet and blowing into their hands in an attempt to keep warm. They are poorly clad, muffled in ragged clothes, collars turned up and flat caps pulled tight.]

SWEENEY: Weather! Come on Maclean, hurry up for Christ's sake! It's freezing here! When's he supposed to arrive?

GIBB: *[Half-apologetic and obviously the organiser.]* He should have been here fifteen minutes ago. Something must have held him up. He's a busy man, you know, taking classes at night and speaking in St Enoch's Square every Sunday. We should really wait and give him a fair hearing.

MCPHEE: *[Forcefully.]* So are *we* busy men! If he doesn't hurry up I'm off. My wife'll be waiting with the tea and I don't want a row. I want a drink before I get home. *[Looks around.]* If it gets any colder we'll all need some whisky in our bellies.

[There is ironic laughter and more attempts to keep warm. Enter Maclean with his helpers Jimmy MacDougall and Tom Kennedy. They are holding pamphlets. Maclean speaks without notes.]

MACLEAN: Good evening comrades. I'm sorry for the delay. I couldn't get away from school. Some children had to see me about extra work. Thank you for waiting in such terrible weather.

[A grudging murmur goes round at his acknowledgement of their discomfort.]

MCPHEE: Right, come on John, hurry up and let's hear what you've got to say about the diseased meat in this town. That's what we're here for.

GREMOLI: Aye, hurry up and get started. We've to be up at five tomorrow to get in for the early shift. We have to pile on the overtime so we can earn enough to get by in this miserable weather.

GIBB: Come on, Luigi, give him a chance. Let's hear what he's to say. *[Nods.]* Right, John, on you go.

MACLEAN: *[Briskly.]* The comrade there mentioned the poisoned meat. That's something that affects every man, woman and child here in this town. Why do you think these Greenock butchers are selling meat from diseased carcases to the workers and their families? Well, the answer's plain, comrades. There are only a few people involved in controlling the meat trade and they want to make as much profit as they can. *They* don't care about whether or not the meat they sell to you is diseased. But rest assured they are not eating it themselves. They bribe the farmers to say nothing then the manager of the slaughter-house. Once that's in place there's nothing to stop them making as much as they are allowed. One answer lies in this pamphlet we've brought tonight.

[MacDougall and Kennedy begin distributing a pamphlet called "The Greenock Jungle". The workers look at it and back at Maclean. There is a moment's embarrassed silence.]

A man in America called Upton Sinclair wrote a book called "The Jungle" and it tells about the poisoned carcases in Chicago. The same thing's going on in Greenock.

GIBB: *[Embarrassed.]* Not everyone here can read, John. [*Looks around.]*

MACLEAN: *[Without patronising.]* I understand that. But the message is the same. We, the workers, need to control the way in which food is produced and the way it is sold. We should have control over *that* to make sure none of our children dies from eating rotten meat and corrupt butchers don't make a profit out of our basic human need for nourishment. The Local Government Board must appoint an independent inspector for the slaughter-house to protect us and our families and to make sure that the beasts are dealt with humanely.

[There is a murmur of disagreement.]

MCPHEE: Not a chance, Maclean. Not a chance. This is a waste of time. How can *we* get anything like that done? They control everything. They've got it all sewn up. The butchers and the slaughter-houses would never accept an inspector. And even if they did, it would be one of their own kind so that they could control him. Come on, be realistic. They've got the police on their side. They beat us up if they get the chance.

MACLEAN: *[Used to being patient.]* You are correct, comrade. The police are there to protect the interests of those who rule. Karl Marx has said that it does not have to be like this. One day we will be in control of all the things which affect our lives, including the food we eat. *[Uses hands to demonstrate what he means, one placed below the other.]* At the moment we are at the bottom and the Capitalist class is at the top. We work, and the profit from our labour goes to the Capitalist class on top. Marx has said that the day will come when we will be on top. *[Switches hands around.]* Then we will share our own profit for our own benefit. And you are correct again. If violence comes, it will come from them first because they have something to lose. *[He coughs chestily.]* Excuse me, I've been speaking outdoors all this month. Our food, our houses, our health, our education, our jobs: everything which we need for our lives will be in our control. And not for someone else's profit.

GREMOLI: Don't talk daft, Maclean! That really is rubbish! How can we control the food or the jobs or the schools? Do you seriously think they're going to allow us to do that? We might as well be at home than here listening to this tripe!

MACLEAN: *[Again patient.]* Keep faith with yourselves and with people of your own class. Don't put your faith in leaders you never see, leaders who never work beside you. Lead yourselves. Organise a trade union. Once you have strength in your union then you will begin to have some say. All over the world there are people just like you working away for someone else's benefit. Join with them. Think about that world where the sugar cane comes from. Then Greenock folk will no longer have to see their children's lives ruined before they've begun.

SWEENEY: If we organise, we get picked on. The papers tell us it's bad to be in a union, especially a union that fights for anything. They say the employers will look after us better. Everybody reads it in the papers.

MACLEAN: *[Emphatic.]* The papers, the judges, the courts, the employers and the police are all going to be against you. Have faith in the things we produce ourselves. Try to buy the "Cooperative News" and the "Vanguard". Get someone to read them to you. Learn to read at evening classes. We don't want working people to be ignorant.

SWEENEY: No, I don't think so. The bosses have got us where they want us. If we complain, we get sacked and there are thousands coming off the boats from Donegal and coming down from the Highlands ready to take any jobs they can get. It's better to keep what we've got and say nothing.

GIBB: *[To other workers rather than Maclean.]* No, listen to what he's saying. Maybe he's right. Look at the miners in Taff Vale in Wales. They won better conditions for themselves by fighting. If we don't do it for ourselves, then we can't expect anybody else to do it for us. Maybe we should get ourselves organised in a union.

MACLEAN: *[Supportive.]* Do that, and don't worry about the future. In the end, working people all over the world will come together for fair trade. I've been to the Shetland Islands to speak to the fishermen there and I've been to Ireland to talk to the dock workers. Working people don't need to be maimed or poisoned or killed in the name of profit. Take your struggle into the world of politics. Be like the miners. Be represented. Remember that *you* give the Capitalist his lifestyle.

GREMOLI: *[Hostile.]* You'll end up in jail, Maclean. If they took you seriously, they'd have you inside. I'm off, lads, I don't know about you. A few drinks then home. Anybody coming?

GIBB: *[Still trying to defend Maclean.]* No, listen to the man. If we don't believe what he says, then who do we put our faith in? The bosses? The churches? We have to put our faith in sharing with each other or else we're nowhere.

[Enter a policeman, walking slowly. He has a baton and is swinging it by his side.]

GREMOLI: *[Seeing him enter.]* Well, I'm off. It doesn't matter what we do, nothing ever gets better.

POLICEMAN: *[Speaking in a West Highland accent.]* What the Hell's going on here, then? Eh? You? *[Indicates MacDougall with his baton.]*

MACDOUGALL: Nothing. We're packing our stuff away. It's not illegal to have meetings now, is it?

POLICEMAN: *[Aggressively.]* Don't give me any of your snash. Just get yourselves away from these factory gates. *[Pauses while they prepare to leave and adds in a derisory tone.]* It's not another of these daft political meetings, eh? Come on, hurry up and get to Hell out of here.

[The policeman supervises them while the groups disperse. He follows slowly in the same direction, offstage.]

SCENE III

[Summer 1907, Glasgow. The living-room of Maclean's tenement flat at Low Cartcraigs, Pollokshaws. Maclean is sitting reading. The room is sparsely furnished but not uncomfortable. Several chairs are available. Light from the window slants onto MacLean. MacDougall enters with Peter Petroff, an asylum seeker newly escaped from Siberia. Petroff is tired from covert travelling and involvement in political struggle. He is dressed in a motley of borrowed clothes.]

MACDOUGALL: *[Excited.]* Johnnie! It's Peter! Here at last! Just in time for tonight's meeting!

[Petroff advances. Maclean rises to greet him. They embrace. Petroff holds Maclean by the shoulders for a silent moment while the implications of the meeting are absorbed.]

MACLEAN: *[Holding back his emotion.]* Sit down. *[Indicates seats with his hands.]* Tell me how you were treated in Leith. Tell me of your travels here, Peter. Tell me everything.

[Petroff and MacDougall sit. The attention is on Petroff.]

PETROFF: *[Passionately.]* It was terrible, John. I have no money left at all. *[Indicates clothes.]* It had to go on bribery, every rouble. *[Smiling.]* Still, it does not matter now that I am safe in Scotland. It is good to be here to breathe the free air.

MACDOUGALL: *[Sardonically.]* Free! Hah! You've come to the wrong place, Peter. *[Looks at Maclean.]*

MACLEAN: *[Reluctantly.]* Aye, this morning we received bad news from our comrades over the water in Ireland. *[Pauses.]* I was in Belfast last week to speak in support of Jim Larkin and the transport workers who were on strike. The workers were struggling to have their union recognised. *[There is an uneasy silence as Maclean looks at the floor.]*

PETROFF: *[Looks from Maclean to MacDougall.]* What happened?

MACDOUGALL: *[Matter-of-fact tone.]* Fourteen strikers were killed by a Scottish regiment on the streets of Belfast. We don't know how many are injured. We are frightened of open warfare because our people do not have guns. It looks as if they will be crushed.

PETROFF: *[After a pause, understanding.]* It was the same in Russia two years ago. The army had been recruited from the poorest peasants. Those of us not killed by them were sent to the camps in the North. The gulags are terrible. I saw things which should not be done by humans. *[Pauses.]* I was lucky. I had money to bribe the guards and I made my way by troika to Tallinn. Your comrades in Leith treated me very well. *[With sudden passion.]* But remember, John, they cannot keep us down for ever!

MACLEAN: *[Quietly.]* We have been working hard here, Peter, and things seem to be going well. I would agree with you. The revolution has to come. We have to take control. I cannot see any other way.

MACDOUGALL: *[Enthusiastically, in the manner of the politically committed.]* We have two or three meetings every day, and the classes in economics too. New branches and new members everywhere, from Carlisle to Lerwick. Now that there is no work for thousands we are trying to organise the unemployed. They have nothing at all, and for most it means starvation or broken families and the workhouse. We have to keep struggling, Peter, there is nothing else for it.

PETROFF: Things are going well in Germany too. Kautsky is busy organising and speaking. The first big breakthrough could come there!

MACLEAN: *[Leaning forward.]* What about the Catholic and Protestant churches? What kind of resistance is there?

PETROFF: *[Gestures with his hands.]* The usual. They try to warn the people off politics and fill their heads with fears about the future. But when *we* take power, they will dance to our tune, don't worry!

MACLEAN: I am worried about the war which is coming with America, Peter. We have to get people organised *there*, if anywhere. The bosses are building themselves into huge trusts and soon they will be able to protect their own interests all over the world. They are doing it now in Central America. We need one big union over there. We have to *educate* the people about what is really happening to them because if *we* don't, no-one else will.

PETROFF: *[As if with greater knowledge.]* Have faith, John, America will fall to Socialism too. One country after another all over the world. We are winning the battle even though the struggle seems hopeless at times.

MACDOUGALL: Look at Belgium. The people have gone on strike and have won the vote. Once they learned about what was happening in the Congo. We can build on our elected members and push from the inside. We'll have to do it soon, Peter. Africa and Asia will end up plundered if we don't.

MACLEAN: *[Still concerned.]* America is at the back of it all the time. Selling guns to one lot and coffins to the other. The big combines in America are using their hungry immigrants as they like, hiring and firing at will. A new slave system.

MACDOUGALL: *[Looks at watch.]* You can speak tonight, Peter. There will be a good crowd in the Burgh Halls. Let's go now and we'll organise a collection for you.

MACLEAN: We know you need to be up early in the morning, Peter. Have you been able to keep in touch with things in London?

PETROFF: [*Rising to leave with the other two.]* On and off, John. There are many refugees joining together in a Party. I have to be there quickly. *[Exeunt.]*

SCENE IV

[Summer 1908. Maclean's living room as before. Enter Maclean, MacDougall, George Pollok and Robert Blair, two young converts to the creed. MacLean is carrying a box which he places in the middle of the floor. He mounts it and faces the audience. MacDougall stands beside him. Pollok and Blair watch this apprehensively.]

MACLEAN: *[Addressing either side.] This* is how you do it. People have come to hear *you* speak, so be prepared. Have your arguments carefully planned. Know what you are going to say. Always link your words about Marx to the things already happening in the factories and shipyards and mines.

MACDOUGALL: *[Didactically.]* Don't talk about 'dialectical materialism'. Leave that for the ones who come to the evening classes. Tell the people that they are the ones who make the wealth but they don't get an equal share of the profits. They can see that. Emphasise the fact that they need to be involved in the struggle.

MACLEAN: *[Warming to his subject.]* Try and put a joke in if you can. If you hear about something which has affected people locally, use it to your advantage.

POLLOK: *[Still apprehensive.]* I'll never manage to get up and speak in front of people, John. It's all right with people you know, people you trust. But complete strangers! *[He gestures hopelessly with his hands.]*

BLAIR: *[Equally apprehensive.]* It's not easy, John. I even get embarrassed standing up to say something at the meetings *we* have. I always feel folk are watching me, waiting for me to make a mistake and then I start blushing and I *do* make a mistake. I don't think I can go ahead with it. It's not a problem for you, John. You're a teacher. You're doing it every day of the week. I'm not.

MACLEAN: *[Patient.]* Robert, you have to take this very seriously.

Look at the bosses and how they have their sons and daughters educated. They are trained to get up and speak easily and put their point of view. They're not slow to tell working people that they're not producing enough or they're lazy or they're troublemakers or the bosses' interests are the workers' interests or whatever. They have been trained to tell you what suits their own ends. *This* is where we learn to fight back. *Here*, in this room.

MACDOUGALL: And never forget the Law. The Law with all its Latin phrases and difficult language. That language is kept deliberately difficult so that we can't get access to it. The bosses can always pay for lawyers who will put forward careful arguments in their defence. Meanwhile we have no money and we stammer and stutter.

MACLEAN: *[Explaining carefully.]* The secret is to be better at their own game than they are. Know your way around the system built on words. You'll have to in any case, because you're bound to end up in court.

MACDOUGALL: *[Walking around.]* You will get no favours from anyone in the system. But the strength of your own people will give you encouragement even when the struggle is difficult.

MACLEAN: *[Quieter.]* Jimmy's right. The struggle is a bitter one. But all over the world just now working people are stirring and we are part of that marvellous Commonwealth. So try, Robert, come up and try.

BLAIR: *[Embarrassed, faltering.]* Comrades, first of all, thank you for coming to listen. *[Pauses, looks at the others and back at the audience.]* Eh, as you know, Capitalism is in crisis. *[Looks at others. There is an embarrassed silence.]* I can't do it! *[Steps down.]*

MACLEAN: *[Remounts box, speaks patiently.]* All right, Robert, that's fine for a first try. *[Turns to Pollok.]* Now, George, you have a go. Let's think about the Education Bill which the Liberals are formulating. That's a crucial one for us. *[MacLean steps down and Pollok takes the box.]*

POLLOK: *[Slightly more assured.]* Comrades, first of all thank you for coming to listen. You all know about the Education Bill which is going through Parliament just now. *[Looks to the others then goes on more fluently.]* Well, that's something we should take a keen interest in because the working class are denied the chances and opportunities which education gives. How's that so far?

MACLEAN: Good. Now get on to the main points of the Bill and show how we can use it to our own advantage.

POLLOK: *[Facing audience again.]* To continue, comrades, we must not lose sight of how serious this issue is. The sons and daughters of the working class do not have the chance to go to secondary schools and cannot afford the Universities. *[Breaks off and looks at them.]*

MACDOUGALL: Great! *[Laughs.]* You're doing so well you can speak at the meeting tonight!

POLLOK: *[Stepping down, serious.]* No! I'm not that good!

MACLEAN: *[Laughing, lifting box.]* Come on, let's go and we'll make an early start. There's a lot to be done. *[Exeunt, smiling.]*

***

SCENE V

[Autumn, 1908. A Committee meeting of Eastwood School Board to decide educational policy for the coming session. Pollok and MacDougall are elected Socialist representatives. The local minister Murdo MacDonald is present and George Watson the Headmaster is in the chair. They are seated around a table, facing the audience.]

WATSON: *[In a firm manner.]* Well, gentlemen, that's the minutes of the previous meeting approved and we have discussed all the correspondence received over the summer. *[Looks round at each one.]*

If there's no objection then we will pass on to the main business of the night, the recommendations we have from Mr Pollok and Mr MacDougall with regard to educational policy.

MACDONALD: *[Speaks in West Highland accent.]* No objection.

MACDOUGALL: No objection.

POLLOK: No objection.

[Watson looks at each one in turn as they answer.]

WATSON: *[Businesslike.]* Well, the first thing concerns food and clothing in schools. Mr MacDougall?

MACDOUGALL: *[Confidently.]* Yes. I'd like to propose that in Eastwood District we release whatever sum of money is required for the purpose of feeding and clothing our necessitous children. Apart from the children being cold, there are large numbers who do not have a nutritious meal each day and it is now our statutory to provide this.

MACDONALD: *[Throughout, he speaks slowly, deliberately and exactly in the manner of a man used to getting his own way.]* Since when was it our financial responsibility to provide food and clothing for *these* children?

WATSON: Under the terms of the new Education Act, Mr MacDonald, we now have the statutory power to feed and clothe deserving children.

MACDONALD: *[Without raising his voice.]* But the cost of this will be extortionate. Where's that kind of money going to come from? The people of Eastwood District will want to ask that question.

MACDOUGALL: The burden of the expense will be borne by the government, through higher taxes as necessary.

[There is an expectant silence.]

MACDONALD: Well, I for one am against this. It says in The Book that The Lord will provide. That is what I will be telling my congregation.

WATSON: *[In a dry manner, as if he has heard MacDonald many times before.]*
It also says in The Book "whoso shall receive one such little child in my name receiveth me", Mr MacDonald. Any further comment?

POLLOK: *[Supportive.]* I would like to endorse everything Mr MacDougall has said.

MACDONALD: Against. People are happy without this sort of extra burden. I will make sure that all of the Highlanders in my congregation vote against this waste of money. Irish Catholics will be the only ones to benefit.

WATSON: *[Firmly.]* I'll have to go along with Mr MacDougall and Mr Pollok since it is, after all, Government policy. *[Writes as he speaks.]* "Henceforth, Eastwood District will provide food and clothing for any deserving pupil in its jurisdiction." Next item. *[He reads.]* "Free books in schools." *[He looks up.]* Mr Pollok?

POLLOK: *[Fluently and precisely.]* Yes, I would like to propose that in Eastwood District we provide free school books for all pupils who cannot afford them. Books unlock the riches of the world. As in the previous item, there should be no regard to cost.

MACDONALD: *[Catching on quickly.]* I suppose this is part of the provision of the new Education Act also? *[Faces MacDougall and Pollok.]* Yes, I can see what you Socialists are up to. Well, I object, but I can see that my objections are going to be useless tonight. *[Indicates the minute book with his forefinger.]* Register my objection please, Mr Watson.

WATSON: Any further comment?

MACDOUGALL: *[Supportive.]* I would like to endorse everything Mr Pollok has said.

WATSON: *[Looks at MacDonald.]* Again, since this is in the terms of the new Act I must go along with Government policy and support Mr MacDougall and Mr Pollok. *[Writes as he speaks.]* "Henceforth Eastwood District will provide free books for any child who cannot afford those books for school purposes." Next item. *[He reads.]* "Free medical examinations and summer sanatoria." Mr MacDougall?

MACDOUGALL: *[Buoyant.]* I would like to propose that all pupils in the charge of Eastwood District are given free medical examinations at least twice in each school year to ensure they have every opportunity to grow up healthy and strong. Good health should not be linked to profit. Free summer camps will help the children take advantage of fresh air and help eradicate tuberculosis. *[Watson glances at MacDonald.]*

MACDONALD: *[Waving him away with his hand.]* The undeserving poor will soon get tired of fresh air and scenery. *[Dryly.]* I should know. I come from Lewis and I have seen the sinners firsthand. Register my objection.

WATSON: Any further comment?

POLLOK: *[Laughingly.]* I would like to support Mr MacDougall in what he has said.

WATSON: *[Objectively.]* Although I have some reservations about the summer camps, I will go along with this item. I have learned to have doubts about certain things. However, the terms of the new Act have to be followed as closely as possible so… *[speaks as he writes]* "Henceforth, Eastwood District will provide free medical examinations twice yearly for all its pupils and summer sanatoria will be established to allow children access to the nearby countryside during the long holiday." Now on to the next item of the night. "Provision of requested continuation classes." Mr Pollok?

POLLOK: *[Confident as before.]* Yes, under the terms of the new Act, School Boards have to provide continuation classes –

MACDONALD: *[Interrupting, mocking.]* The people of the South Side want to watch football at night.

POLLOK: *[Continuing forcefully.]* Classes requested by more than twenty people *[holds up a list]* and I have twenty one names here. I would like to propose that Eastwood School Board inaugurates a class in Economics this winter. I would also like to propose that the tutor of the class be John Maclean-

WATSON: *[Genuinely surprised.]* Maclean!

POLLOK: *[Calm.]* John Maclean, and that Karl Marx be the main author studied.

MACDONALD: *[With rising anger.]* Maclean and Marx! No. Register my objections immediately. I will do everything in my power, use all my contacts, exert all my influence to make sure this does not come to pass. All decent, Scottish people will righteously rebel against this sick dogma. Godless people! Register my objection, Watson, and register that I left the meeting early without taking part in a debate which suggests there is no God! *[Rises to leave. Remarks directly to Pollok and MacDougall.]* I am going from this meeting to talk with the editor of the Church newspaper. You will not be getting away with this. I will even be prepared to talk to the Roman Catholics. *[Exit. Silence till he goes.]*

WATSON: John Maclean. I am surprised to hear that name mentioned, gentlemen. I happen to know this person's record and, principled as he might appear, I could not support this appointment at all. It would never be acceptable to the people of this community. No, I am afraid I cannot go along with this.

POLLOK: *[Sticking to wording of Act.]* The request is entirely within the terms of the Act. This list is completely genuine, Mr Watson. Since you have supported the other items I would suggest that you could not rationally deny your support to this one.

MACDOUGALL: Yes, Mr Pollok and I are both in agreement. That is two to one *[looks towards door]* with one abstention.

WATSON: *[Speaking stiffly, writing.]* “Henceforth, Eastwood District will provide continuation classes of any kind which are requested by groups of people numbering twenty or more. The first Economics class will be tutored by John Maclean and Karl Marx will be the main author studied. *[Pauses while he completes his writing.]* One more item tonight. Mr MacDougall.

MACDOUGALL: Yes, I’ll keep it brief. Eastwood District should abolish all Bible teaching in secular schools. As well as this, bursaries should be provided for all young people who wish to go on to colleges and universities.

WATSON: *[Realising the futility of argument.]* The two are unrelated.

MACDOUGALL: It doesn’t matter. Reform is long overdue.

WATSON: I must oppose on grounds of conscience.

POLLOK: I support Mr MacDougall.

WATSON: *[Writing as he speaks.]* “Henceforth Eastwood District Council will abolish Bible teaching in secular schools and will provide bursaries for all who wish to go on to post-school education.” *[Pauses till he finishes.]* Well gentlemen, I think that concludes the business of the evening. I will be submitting the minutes to the press for information purposes. *[Pauses.]* You have been successful *tonight*, gentlemen. *[He rises from his seat.]* Goodnight.

MACDOUGALL: *[Rising, obviously pleased.]* Goodnight!

POLLOK: *[Rising, laughing.]* Goodnight!

[Exeunt Pollok and MacDougall, talking in an animated way. Watson waits behind, looking at his papers, thinking. The light fades on him.]

END OF ACT ONE

***

ACT TWO

SCENE I

[December 1908. Outside the gates of Stobhill Hospital, Glasgow. Maclean, dressed formally as before, is also wearing a hat and a warm, unbuttoned overcoat. It is a clear night, cold, sharp and fresh. Maclean is enjoying the tranquillity of the moment while he waits for his fiancée, Agnes Wood, who is a nurse. He is beneath a gas lamp. Agnes enters. She is pretty although her features suggest severity. She is in reality very shy and retiring with outsiders. Agnes is holding her coat collar tightly round her throat to fend off the cold. A hat hugs her head closely. In her free hand she is carrying a letter.]

AGNES: *[Slightly breathless. She speaks in a Borders accent.]* John! You're there! I'm sorry I'm late! Nurse MacKay has contracted pneumonia and we're really short-staffed. Meg and I had to look after the beds till Matron could switch someone from a quieter ward. *[Suddenly shy, tender and secret.]* How are you? *[They kiss.]*

MACLEAN: *[Relishes the kiss. Looks at her pleased.]* Fine, Agnes, fine and I'm enjoying the night better now. *[Laughs and indicates letter.]* Is that word from your Uncle James?

AGNES: *[Inwardly glad.]* Aye, it is John. *[Holds letter out.]* He sends his regards to you and says he gives us his blessing. *[She takes the letter from the envelope and they move closer to the pool of light from the gas lamp.]* Here's the bit, John. *[She reads.]* "Of course I give you my blessing, Agnes. You've been more than a daughter to me and I'm glad you've got a man of John's character to make you happy." *[Breaks off, emotional.]* That's important to me, John. *[Reads on.]* "Tell John I'm asking for him. He made quite an impression in Hawick although I don't think some of them are ready for his brand of Marxism yet. Still, we've got the Social Reform Society on the go, and the weavers are proving strong supporters, just as John predicted. It's up to you to make sure he knows there are things in life which are better and more important than politics. And tell him I've made him a new pair of leather brogues to help keep his feet warm when he's tramping the streets this winter. I'll give them to you for him when I see you at the New Year." *[She breaks off again.]* Are you pleased too, John?

MACLEAN: *[Laughing.]* Of course I am. I like the bit where he says I should leave time for you. *[Holds her to him.]* We are going to be together all the time now, my love. *[Kisses her passionately. They break off and there is a silence as they consider the implications of their impending marriage.]*

AGNES: *[Worried.]* Will we be all right for money, John? Can we afford it?

MACLEAN: *[Placating her.]* Of course we'll be all right. I've got my regular money from teaching and a bit saved by. We will be able to get a house of our own somewhere near my mother in Pollokshaws and you can get a tram straight through.

AGNES: *[Still worried.]* Your job, though, John. Look what happened to Jimmy MacDougall.

MACLEAN: *[In a changed tone.]* Jimmy's all right now! There's enough money coming in from public collections and from the pamphlets to pay him a wage. And anyway, it's better with him working full time for the revolution. I wish it was me!

AGNES: *[Insistent.]* *I* would rather have you teaching full time. That way we can plan for *our* future. I don't mind helping with the organization whenever I can. But I don't want *you* getting into trouble at work. They can make things very difficult.

MACLEAN: *[Not willing to continue.]* The worst they can do is transfer me. They daren't sack me because of the outcry there would be. There's a shortage of teachers. And you know I never let my political work interfere with what I do in the classroom.

AGNES: The Bible?

MACLEAN: That blew over. You want a secure future. That's what I want for everybody, including us. I look at the system that spends money on weapons of mass destruction. I worry about America and her Trusts. I think about wars conducted in the name of religion. That's why I want to be full time, to speak against those horrors.

AGNES: *[Not giving in.]* If the slum landlords can get Jimmy removed from the Bank for opposing their racketeering then the Kirk can get rid of you. Don't think John MacLean is more powerful than the Kirk.

MACLEAN: *[Defiant.]* The ironmoulders in Falkirk withdrew their money from the Clydesdale. The Bank didn't like that. And Jimmy's getting big numbers in his classes, especially in Fife and Ayrshire.

AGNES: *[Still insistent.]* This business at the Neilston Thread Mill. Are you going to put yourself out for that?

MACLEAN: *[Reluctant.]* Of course I'm going to support them. The bosses want cheap, non-union labour. Especially women. You yourself told me that babies are dying in there *[nods back to hospital]* because there's not enough money being spent on health care. We need one big union of thread-workers and nurses and ship-builders and miners to beat sweated labour. That's why I *must* get involved.

AGNES: *[Appealing directly to him.]* I don't want your vision to spoil our life together, John.

MACLEAN: *[More satisfied.]* It won't Agnes, don't worry. There's enough money for us to get married. Write back and tell your Uncle James I promise to spend all my time outside meetings with you. And tell him to make sure the shoes don't fall to bits after a month.

AGNES: *[Folding away the letter.]* Aye, I'll tell him. *[She links his arm.]* Right, Mr Maclean, that's enough of the arguing. I'll let you see me home tonight now – on one condition.

MACLEAN: *[Glad the friction has passed.]* Aye, Miss Wood, and what condition would that be? *[Holding her close.]*

AGNES: *[Deliberately.]* That you accompany me to Rouken Glen tomorrow on my afternoon off and that you walk me to the waterfall.

MACLEAN: Oh, I don't know about that. I'll have to see if I have any previous engagements with some pretty women I know.

AGNES: John!

MACLEAN: *[Laughing. Puts his arms around her.]* Come on! We might manage a walk in the park before the night's out.

[Exeunt, the lovers kissing and holding each other close.]

***

SCENE II

[Spring 1909. A Masonic Club on the south side of Glasgow. Symbols and insignia are in evidence. Enter four Masons, carrying drinks. They have just finished a meal and have already been drinking quite heavily. There is laughter and banter as they light cigars and settle around a table, facing the audience. Charles Diamond, the director of the English Sewing Company, owners of the Neilston Thread Mill, is middle-aged and portly enough to be bulging out of his three-piece suit. Ian Fergusson is a solicitor and notary public in Glasgow. He has a perceptive insight. Ewan Campbell is a local branch manager of the Clydesdale Bank, a man sensitive to the links between money and power. Calum Innes, a Highland police sergeant, is powerfully built, cunning but not intellectual. He has seen human behaviour in all its unpleasant vagaries and knows that he is well-off in the position he occupies.]

FERGUSSON: *[Superficially friendly.]* Congratulations, Charles. You'll do well in the Craft. Keep your nose clean and you can go very high. It won't do you any harm at all to be in with us.

DIAMOND: *[Eagerly.]* Thank you, Ian. I'm really glad it's over. I've been rehearsing my responses for months now. I was pleased everything went to plan. I was scared I might make a mistake! *[Laughs nervously.]*

INNES: *[Mocking.]* Like not calling my men in to help you against Maclean's army?

[The others laugh. Diamond is uneasy.]

CAMPBELL: *[Smugly at first.]* I'd like to hear the full story about that. *[More seriously.]* I've had some trouble myself recently.

DIAMOND: *[Facing a critical, worldly audience.]* I didn't really have much room for manoeuvre. There were hundreds of them outside the house singing and shouting. Banging bin lids and tins off the ground and that fool Maclean shouting about Unions and Socialism. *[Pauses.]* I agreed to discussions about wages and said I'd refer the matter about Unions to a committee in the works.

FERGUSSON: You mean you lost out to Maclean?

DIAMOND: *[Defensive.]* No. Not at all. Pollokshields is a quiet area. I had to get rid of them quickly. The neighbours. *[More glibly.]* Anyway, profits are high just now and I'll soon make it up. Their wages are related to piece work and overtime and I've told the foremen not to replace any women who leave to have children. I pay the women less. The foremen will be in the Unions so they will know what's going on.

FERGUSSON: *[Pressing.]* You don't think these Unions will come to anything?

DIAMOND: *[Beginning to relax.]* No. We can starve them out if they stop production. Female labour is cheaper and there are plenty of hungry families in Neilston and Barrhead and Paisley. Show me one vacancy and I'll show you a hundred ready to fill it. We had the whole thing under control. We didn't need Calum's men.

INNES: *[Contentedly.]* We were ready, you know. Some of my boys are itching to get a crack at the Reds. We owe them one or two.

FERGUSSON: *[Directing.]* I'm not so sure about these Unions. I've been reading articles about them. *[The others defer to his position.]* It would seem that there are the same agitations in Europe and America and not just here on the Clyde. I've also read some of this Karl Marx.

CAMPBELL: *[Knowing that Fergusson is an intellectual.]* Why? Why have you done that?

FERGUSSON: *[With a tinge of sarcasm.]* You're the money man. You should know. We will need brains as well as brawn to disrupt them. We will need the newspapers on our side to show the workers every day what a useless doctrine this Socialism is. *[Pauses to take a drink.]* We'll only bring in Calum and then the courts when we're losing the arguments. Take out the ringleaders with their energy and the whole thing falls apart. It's easy to provoke a violent response.

INNES: *[Pleased to be able to display his cunning.]* I already have a few of my own men mixing with these hotheads. Two of my most experienced officers follow Maclean around. They report on what is said and who is present and how much money changes hands. That way we can keep ahead of things.

[The others signal their admiration.]

CAMPBELL: The money is going to be an important issue. Some of the wild talk says that they're going to take banks into their own control. Abolish interest and dividends. That's why I had one of Maclean's men dismissed.

FERGUSSON: Why? Have you had bother?

CAMPBELL: *[Slightly reluctant.]* All the usual crowd, the Irish, the Co-operatives, the Liberals and the whole rag-bag were making noises about Sim. Shouting about high rents and racketeering and trying to get repairs done or have the buildings shut. Sim banks with us and I didn't want him moving the account somewhere else. One of the agitators was a MacDougall, an apprentice clerk. I got rid of him. The bother soon died down.

FERGUSSON: *[Sharp.]* Ah! Was that linked to the business in Falkirk?

CAMPBELL: *[Again reluctant.]* Up there the Union members withdrew their deposits. But they had so little and Sim's account was worth a hundred times as much. It was another token, futile gesture.

INNES: *[Becoming slightly bored.]* Right lads, enough about Marx and Unions and Maclean. We'll get him if we have to so stop worrying. Charles. A toast to you in the hope that you always fulfil your duties faithfully. *[Raises his glass.]* Charles!

[The others drink the toast.]

DIAMOND: *[Flushed.]* Drink up, men. This is my night tonight and I want to enjoy every moment of it. If I can help you or your families or your businesses in any way just let me know. I'm proud to be part of the Craft and I aim to be true to it till the day I die.

[Diamond signals to the bar and the others settle back in a satisfied manner. The lights fade on them.]

***

SCENE III

[Summer 1911. A mining club in the Rhondda Valley. A table is set facing an audience of miners who have just heard H.M. Hyndman, founder of the Social Democratic Foundation, debate against Maclean. The chairman brings the meeting to a close using a gavel. The voices gradually quieten.]

CHAIRMAN: Order, comrades. You have had the chance to hear both speakers at length. I will read the motion one last time and then comrade Hyndman and comrade Maclean will give brief conclusions before we proceed to the vote. *[Lifts piece of paper and reads slowly.]* "That the Rhondda miners vote to increase coal production to new Government-established levels so that extra steel for the refurbishment of the Royal Navy can be produced." *[Puts paper on table and looks over his glasses at Hyndman.]* Comrade Hyndman.

HYNDMAN: *[Rises to polite applause.]* Three main points, comrades. Jobs. Peace. Freedom. In recent years you and your families have faced the same problems with regard to steady employment in the mines. If you support this resolution, jobs for you and your sons will be guaranteed for at least the next four years. The amount of steel needed by the Government will be agreed and we can work out the coal required for that amount. It is likely that extra jobs will be created. Peace, comrades, is never easily gained. Many of you here have fought in South Africa. We all know that within Germany there are groups who want war in Europe. How can we help our comrades in Europe? The answer is simple. The coal we produce will make the steel which the Navy needs to make it the biggest and most powerful in the world. This will stop the Germans from thinking about invading other countries. And lastly, freedom, comrades. Most other countries are not lucky enough to have as many basic rights and freedoms as we have. These rights have to be defended and we do not want the Welsh to be called unpatriotic. We have to defend the British way of life at all costs. So do that comrades! Vote for this resolution, be patriotic, remain free, protect jobs, earn wages and keep this world peaceful!

[He sits down with a flourish. There is steady applause.]

CHAIRMAN: *[Rises and taps table with gavel. Nods at Hyndman.]* Thank you, comrade, for those words. Now comrade Maclean will give his conclusion before the vote. *[Nods to MacLean.]*

MACLEAN: Comrades. This Government has no money for the social reforms we desperately need. No money for health care, no money for education, no money for housing, no money to help unemployment. But when a war is coming, they can pull any amount out of the hat because war means profit! There is a lot of money to be made out of the working classes of the world killing each other. Bombs, guns, ammunition, clothes, boots, food, tents, horses, leather, cigarettes, drink, transport, coffins: the list is endless and the bosses will make profits out of it all. Freedom? Look around you here in the Rhondda. Democracy? Patriotism? You people are the poorest of the poor. The other workers of the world are your brothers, not your enemies. I stand here and say I am ashamed of my own country. Scottish regiments off killing all around the world. We have no reason to go and kill another person because he was born in a different culture. If the class struggle is to succeed, the workers of the world must be united, not divided against each other. It is much harder to make peace across the nations than to make war. We have to reject this resolution. Have nothing to do with the warmongers! Vote for resolutions which will improve the lives of all the people. There must be no more war! *[Maclean sits.]*

[There is scattered applause.]

CHAIRMAN: *[Stands, obtains silence. Nods to Maclean.]* Thank you, comrade Maclean. Now comrades, we proceed at once to the vote on this resolution. All those in favour. *[The miners vote. The Chairman counts.]* Those against. *[The miners vote. The Chairman counts.]* The resolution is narrowly carried. *[The Chairman shakes hands with Hyndman and Maclean. They collect their papers and exeunt.]*

***

SCENE IV

[Late January 1915. Maclean's living room in his small house in Auldhouse Road, Glasgow. Maclean is sitting in an armchair beside the fire writing, while Agnes sets the table for the evening meal. She passes to and fro before the conversation begins. There is an unpleasant tension between them.]

AGNES: *[Without looking at him.]* Well?

MACLEAN: *[Without looking at her.]* Well what?

AGNES: Are you going to or are you *not* going to?

MACLEAN: *[Obtuse.]* Am I going to what or am I not going to what?

AGNES: *[Slamming a saucer on the table.]* Stop being awkward, John! Are you going to give up this useless campaigning against the war?

MACLEAN: *[Deliberately.]* No.

[There is further silence between them.]

AGNES: *[Trying another tack.]* You haven't been able to prevent the war and you're not going to end it a day earlier.

MACLEAN: *[Continuing to write.]* Who *is* going to end it a day earlier?

AGNES: *[Frustrated.] I* don't know but *I'm* the one who has to live with you day in and day out and see you getting old before your time. *[Maclean refuses to answer.]* I want you to spend some time with me away from this eternal round of politics. We could go away for a day or two together, like we used to. *[Again he refuses to answer.]* You need a rest yourself, John. You've been speaking every night since the war started. Your throat has been sore. *[Pauses.]* And you're worried that the school authorities are trying to get rid of you. *[Again he refuses to acknowledge her and continues to write.]* John!

MACLEAN: *[Looks up.]* What is it?

AGNES: *[Stands holding cutlery and shouts in desperation.]* Stop acting like this and answer me! I want you to spend a bit more time with me!

MACLEAN: *[Hardened.]* I can't give you the answer you want.

AGNES: Why not?

MACLEAN: *[Matter-of-fact.]* Last week thousands of people from my class were slaughtered on an obscure field in France. That's why not. *[He resumes writing.]*

AGNES: Everyone else is supporting the war. The T.U.C., the Co-operative movement and the Labour Party. Are you some kind of martyr? The French Socialists have voted to fight for democracy. Your friend Sembat. Remember?

MACLEAN: *[Puts pen down, getting angry.]* This is about betrayal! Hyndman. Kautsky. Plekhanov. Vaillant. I'm not the one who's wrong! If Jim Connolly and I don't keep fighting then there's nothing! Nothing! *[Crumples his paper in anger and stands angrily in the room.]*

AGNES: You can't stop the war, John! They won't even let you *speak* at meetings in London and Wales!

MACLEAN: To Hell with London and Wales! This is the Clyde and it's different here! The people on the streets know they can trust us! *[Pauses.]* Agnes, you and I are happily married, aren't we?

AGNES: *[Reluctantly. Looks away and sets table.]* Yes.

MACLEAN: Imagine I was fighting in France. Would you not be happier knowing that there was somebody back at home trying to bring this war to an end? I'm sure the wives of the soldiers and sailors want that. And when the soldiers and sailors are killed, the families are being left in poverty. I've got to keep writing and I've got to keep speaking. *[Agnes is still unmoved. Maclean looks anew at her, realising he has been neglecting her.]* Agnes!

AGNES: *[Looks up.]* What?

MACLEAN: *[Calmer now.]* You're right, Agnes. I am tired. Let me write these few things and let me speak at Weir's, Atlas and Parkhead Forge. We have to convince the munitions workers. Let me do that this week and then on Saturday we'll go away. *[He moves to hold her.]*

AGNES: *[Her voice still showing restraint.]* Where to?

MACLEAN: You name a place!

AGNES: No. You make a promise.

MACLEAN: All right. We'll go to Rothesay for the day. We'll get the benefit of the sail.

[They hold each other and kiss.]

AGNES: *[Still with an element of doubt.]* Promise? We'll go to Rothesay this Saturday?

MACLEAN: I promise, Agnes.

[They hug as the lights fade, but the tension is not fully resolved.]

***

SCENE V

[Summer 1915. Evening in the hot and smoky office of a London newspaper. The editor and sub-editor are checking the final pages of copy before it goes to press. They now have to decide what should take priority on the next morning's front page.]

EDITOR: *[Exhaling smoke, wearily.]* What do you think yourself?

SUB: *[Scanning choices.]* The picture of the field guns and the report from the war correspondent. *[Reads.]* "The Germans, tremendously reinforced, endeavoured to break through at Ypres last week. Part of the British line was compelled to retire temporarily, leaving six guns in an exposed position. There was not a moment to lose. Who should bring in those guns? Artillery men and infantrymen at once responded to the call and dashed out on the perilous errand. Two of the weapons were saved under the eyes of the enemy. German shells fell thick and fast round the men whose very contempt of danger seemed to act as a charm against injury."

EDITOR: [*Obviously unsatisfied.]* What else is there?

SUB: An illustration of a group of Cossacks standing beside some corpses. *[Reads.]* "German brutality is not confined to their western operations. On the eastern frontier dastardly atrocities have also been committed. Trumpeters of German culture denounced England for allying itself with Russia, whose Cossacks, they asserted, were rank barbarians. Yet, while the Germans cut off the hands and ears of wounded Cossacks the Russian soldiers themselves are forbidden, under pain of death, to molest non-combatants, or to pillage."

EDITOR: Yes. That's much better. I don't want any bad feelings about Ypres. We must promote the Russians as natural allies. Right. That sounds like the lead story and sketch. What else?

SUB: A piece on the Munitions Act. Ministers have suggested to me we should be helping them more. The same with conscription.

EDITOR: [*Stubs out cigarette.]* Have we got anything we can use about conscription?

SUB: This fellow Maclean has been doing a bit of rabble-rousing around the country. At least, where he's been allowed to speak. Word is he's just been arrested. *[Looks up.]*

EDITOR: *[Interested.]* Yes. John Maclean. The Ministers are not happy with him. What's the charge?

SUB: [*Glancing at notes.]* Using language likely to cause a breach of the peace. Apparently there are thousands come to hear him at open-air meetings.

EDITOR: Have we got anything we can use against him?

SUB: There's a draft here. *[Reads.]* "Glasgow Red Financed By Kaiser's Gold".

EDITOR: That's quite good. Get words like "traitor" and "conspiracy" in. Don't give too many facts. Just say he's been arrested, his trial will be taking place soon and we can do without his kind not helping our boys at the Front. Say he's had the white feather thrown at him.

SUB: *[Scribbling.]* Is that true?

EDITOR: Doesn't matter. I've got a feeling he will cause us more trouble before he's finished. Find out who his enemies on the Left are so we can exploit that in future. Divide and rule and all that. Conscription will come, you know.

SUB: *[Still scribbling.]* What makes you say that?

EDITOR: Too many heavy losses on the Front. Sea losses have been just as heavy but we will have to do something on mainland Europe.

SUB: *[Looking up.]* Putting over conscription will not be an easy one.

EDITOR: Articles like that will help. We have to discredit the anti-war people and the conscientious objectors. Now what else? Royalty?

SUB: George and his duty to "his very dear people".

EDITOR: Put it in. Is that the front page just about filled?

SUB: I'll get it down to the case-room straight away. I'll stay on and tidy up.

EDITOR: That would be a help. I'm at breakfast with Lloyd George then at dinner with the Ulster Unionists. I'll see you tomorrow evening before we go to press. God! This war's a dreary business! *[Stands and yawns.]*

SUB: Goodnight, sir.

EDITOR: Goodnight. *[Exit as the lights fade.]*

END OF ACT TWO

***

ACT THREE

SCENE I

[December 1915. St Andrew's Halls, Glasgow. Lloyd George, Minister of Munitions, has come to Glasgow to promote dilution of labour as a prelude to conscription. On the platform are Maclean, Arthur Henderson as Chairman and David Kirkwood, convener of Shop Stewards. The platform party is standing while the assembled munitions workers finish singing "The Red Flag".]

HENDERSON: *[Indicates that all should sit.]* Comrades. Good morning and welcome to this very important meeting. I am delighted to have the opportunity of appearing in St Andrew's Halls with Mr Lloyd George, Minister of Munitions…

MUNITIONS WORKER: *[Interrupting.]* He should be delighted to have the opportunity to speak to us! *[There is laughter and applause from the audience.]*

HENDERSON: *[Continuing.]* …delighted to have Lloyd George as the greatest orator of the Labour movement. Gentlemen, Lloyd George. *[Lloyd George rises to speak. There is stony silence.]*

GEORGE: *[Obviously perturbed and embarrassed at this unusual, irreverent reception.]* Good morning, comrades. It's good to be back in Glasgow where the weather's cold but the hearts are warm! *[There is no response to his attempt at assumed familiarity. He is experienced enough not to continue in this vein.]* Anyway, comrades, I am here today to speak to you about the Munitions Act which seems to be giving rise to groundless concern…

MUNITIONS WORKER: *[Heckling.]* It can't be groundless or else you wouldn't be up here preaching to us! *[There is loud applause and stamping of feet.]*

GEORGE: *[Again, taken aback.]* Well, comrade, I am here to explain to you why you need have no cause for concern. *[He adopts a firm tone.]* You are all aware that we are engaged in probably the greatest war ever…

MUNITIONS WORKER: Aye! The class war! *[There are loud roars of applause.]*

GEORGE: *[Continuing less assuredly.]* …the greatest war that our old country has been concerned with. At this moment the rest of Great Britain is looking to the Clyde for a lead. We are relying on you and your traditional skills to help us in our crusade for freedom against these German assassins of democracy! What the soldiers need is munitions, not strikes!

MUNITIONS WORKER: Rubbish! Are you prepared to give the workers a controlling say in the management of the munitions factories?

GEORGE: *[Nervous at this development.]* That doesn't really concern us this morning. We can come back to that later. Now to go on…

MUNITIONS WORKER: Shame! Answer the man! Will the workers have a controlling say in the management of the factories?

GEORGE: At the moment I couldn't say one way or another. That wouldn't be a decision for any one individual. That would have to be referred to a committee.

MUNITIONS WORKER: Come on, George, give us a straight answer. You're supposed to be the big shot everybody listens to.

GEORGE: *[Increasingly ruffled.]* As I have said, comrade, that's not a decision for any one individual but rest assured that the Clydeside workers will be the first to know of any decision which is reached.

[There are mocking groans at this ineptitude from a much-vaunted speaker.]

HENDERSON: *[Standing.]* Come on comrades. Be reasonable. Give the man a chance to speak. We haven't heard the rest of what he has to tell us!

MUNITIONS WORKER: We've heard enough already! *[There is more laughter and applause.]*

GEORGE: *[Struggling.]* To move on, comrades. I want to examine the great issue at the moment as far as the war is concerned…

MUNITIONS WORKER: Profit! *[There are further roars.]*

GEORGE: *[Provoked into anger now.]* No! Not profits! The defence of freedom and the British way of life!

[There are loud groans of disbelief. The munitions workers begin the slow handclap and stamp their feet. Lloyd George looks to a powerless Henderson. Kirkwood confers with Maclean then stands and appeals for silence. The noise subsides.]

KIRKWOOD: Comrades. Comrades. Unfortunately it is the feeling of the meeting that Lloyd George should be regarded with a great deal of suspicion. This seems to be based on the fact that every Act with which his name is associated has some semblance of slavery about it. *[There are roars of approval. Lloyd George is visibly disturbed at this development.]* However, comrade Maclean has agreed to address the meeting. *[Loud applause greets this.]* Comrade Maclean.

MACLEAN: *[At the height of his influence.]* Comrades. You have heard enough from the great Lloyd George to know that he is just another paid lackey from a London Government. *[Loud applause.]* You have noticed the fact which has escaped him that there will be no Trade Union rights under this Munitions Act. He wants to conscript the men and fill their places with cheap, female labour. As a Socialist, I say that I cannot accept this. Women will come to play a decisive role in society's development and will no longer be denied their rightful position in a democratic country. Every woman's influence will come to humanise mankind which is wallowing in filth and beastliness! *[Loud applause.]* And I say to you, comrades, and I tell Lloyd George to take this message back to London. There must be no conscription! We on the Clyde reject being the chattel slaves of William Weir and Herr Krupps. And we will use the weapon of strike action to make sure this Government knows that we mean what we say! Lloyd George is right when he says one thing. The rest of Britain *is* looking to the Clyde for a lead. A lead in saying that there must be an end to this mad slaughter! And to this end here and now we send greetings to our comrades in Russia who are engaged in the war we *should* be fighting – the class war! *[There is roaring, clapping and shouts of support.]* The peasants of Russia are going to show us our future! This is our message to London! No more war! Long live the revolution!

[Maclean sits down. There is anarchic applause which develops by turn into a singing of "The Red Flag". Lloyd George, gravely perturbed, watches this display as the lights fade.]

***

SCENE II

[February 1916. The military section of Edinburgh Castle where Maclean is a prisoner. There is total silence at first. Maclean is sitting alone in his cell, holding his head in his hands and looking at the floor. The noise of keys jangling, locks opening and closing and iron doors slamming can be heard. A prison warder enters, bringing Maclean his evening meal on a tray.]

MACLEAN: Well?

WARDER: *[Abruptly.]* Well what?

MACLEAN: *[Rising to take food tray and sitting again.]* Am I to be allowed to see Petroff?

WARDER: *[Looking down at him.]* No.

MACLEAN: Why not?

WARDER: *[Laughs.]* The word is that your Russian pal is an alien and he'll shortly be sailing out of Leith on his merry way back to where he came from.

MACLEAN: *[Obviously upset.]* Is that correct? Who told you?

WARDER: I don't know if it's correct or not. There are too many rumours fly about this place. I just do what I'm told, take my pay and go home. What I *do* know is that you've not to see Petroff. Satisfied?

[Maclean eats and refuses to answer. The warder is taking some delight in being able to torment such a famous person.]

The paper was saying today that you and your cronies get money from The Kaiser. Is that right?

MACLEAN: No. Someone sits in an office and twists stories to suit their own purposes.

WARDER: *[Disbelieving.]* I'm not so sure. *[Pauses.]* You might be getting some company in here soon.

MACLEAN: *[Anxious to know what lies at the root of this.]* Why? Who's been arrested?

WARDER: Ah, now. Some more of your Red pals. Somebody called Gallacher and somebody called Muir. There was a third one as well. I can't remember his name.

MACLEAN: Walter Bell?

WARDER: That sounds familiar. They were saying that the workers should shoot the Government. Surely you don't go along with that as well?

MACLEAN: I'd be wary of saying anything to you in here. You seem to be a bit of a gossip.

WARDER: *[Angry.]* Watch it, Maclean. You could be in here for a long time after what you've been up to. It's penal servitude for a criminal act under the Defence of the Realm Act and there's a few warders in this place can't wait to find out what your sentence will be.

[Maclean refuses to be drawn by this. The warder watches him in silence while he eats.]

Who's looking after your wife and kids?

MACLEAN: The workers. Until the trial date on April the eleventh. Then we'll see what happens.

WARDER: The workers? What do you mean?

MACLEAN: *[Painfully.]* Money is collected at meetings and enough is sent to my wife to help her get by. We'll manage.

WARDER: *[Laughs.]* Who's going to speak in your defence at the trial?

MACLEAN: Why? Do you know the names of any decent people in this country?

WARDER: *[Glad that Maclean is being riled.]* The ones I read about in the papers.

MACLEAN: James Maxton will speak for me. So will Mannie

Shinwell. Helen Crawford. John Cassells will defend me and he's not even a Socialist.

WARDER: *[Continuing to aggravate.]* There are eighteen police officers going to testify against you.

MACLEAN: *[Not to be broken.]* I'm surprised they could find one who understood the speech.

WARDER: You won't be making wisecracks like that in front of the Lord Advocate. Do you know what it's like in the Calton Jail?

MACLEAN: *[Hesitant.]* No. [Pauses.] Do you?

WARDER: *[Settling into the role of raconteur.]* I worked there for a couple of years. There are some hard, hard men on the staff. Mostly ex-police or from the mental hospitals. They'll keep *you* in order.

MACLEAN: What about books?

WARDER: What *about* books? You get none. No paper. No pens. No fags. *[He laughs ironically.]* The food's good after a while, though. Then there's the silence, the isolation and the no-talk rule. *You* might even be lucky enough to get Peterhead.

MACLEAN: *[Anxious.]* What's the difference?

WARDER: Plenty of fresh air up there. You work outside in all weathers in the penal gangs. It's a cold wind that blows from Norway.

MACLEAN: How many times would I get to see my wife?

WARDER: *[Taking the tray back.]* One pass every two months.

MACLEAN: How long for?

WARDER: Two hours. Depends on the delays with travel. *[Prepares to leave.]* Anyway. I'm glad I'm too old for conscription. All the young lads are lining up ready to go to the war. A bit of discipline will do them good. That's my shift finished. Off home. Quick pint and back in front of the fire for my tea. Probably see you tomorrow. *[Exit.]*

MACLEAN: Goodnight.

WARDER: Goodnight.

[There are sounds of cells being locked and the retreat of the warder into the distance. Maclean sits staring at the walls of his cell. The lights go out on him.]

***

SCENE III

[July 1917. The living-room of Maclean's house in Auldhouse Road, Glasgow. Maclean is sitting in his armchair reading. Agnes is as before, preparing the table for a meal. Maclean has aged visibly, older and greyer. Agnes' face shows the strain of having lived with a prisoner for a husband. There is tension in the air again. They are continuing a conversation which has been broken off.]

AGNES: *[Arranging plates.]* And what about the *judge's* comments? You can't ignore them.

MACLEAN: *[Without looking up.]* He made lots of comments which I paid no heed to. He's employed by the system. It's as simple as that.

AGNES: *[Frustrated.]* It's *not* as simple as that! He said that your crime was punishable by death or penal servitude. Remember that I had to live with the worry of *that*.

MACLEAN: *[Flat.]* When the revolution comes here, in Scotland, no-one will suffer from judgements like that again. I'm just a small, insignificant cog in the wheels of history. Others will take my place. *[He continues reading.]*

AGNES: *[Exploding.]* Insignificant! You're my husband! The father of our two children! How can you turn round and say this! Don't be a fool! When the judge said "death" he meant *death*!

MACLEAN: *[Defiant.]* I don't care what the judge said. The end is coming for him and his kind.

AGNES: *[Angry.]* Look what has happened to the others! Don't refuse to see what's all around you. They tied Jim Connolly to a chair and shot him eight times! That's what the brutes did! Am I supposed to stand back and watch my husband go the same way?

[Maclean refuses to answer.]

Jim MacDougall has collapsed with a nervous breakdown. A young man like that! He was fit and healthy and strong, Johnnie! They broke him! Look at you! You're old before your time! My husband! Old!

[She turns away at the realisation of this. There is silence for a moment while she composes herself. She resumes the conversation quietly.]

Jimmy Maxton has been dismissed by the School Board. You've lost your job. Johnnie Lennox was killed in France. One week after he was shipped out. His mother will never recover.

MACLEAN: *[Uncomfortable.]* He should never have gone.

AGNES: Ha! That shows how much you know! They were crucifying him! He was watching his parents suffer because there was a "traitor" in the family. He did it for love of them! So *you* should give up *this* for my sake! They brought conscription in anyway. Why should ours be the family which has to make all the sacrifices?

MACLEAN: *[With simmering anger.]* Am I supposed to sit back and let the ones in power do what they like with ordinary people? Krupps is selling his weapons to the Belgians through a neutral state so that German soldiers can be butchered!

AGNES: What about me? You're always on about other people suffering. What about the suffering we've been through? Nan was nearly *killed* with scarlet fever! Then Jean and I were in the isolation ward with it. What about us? I was the one who had to stand there in the Calton Jail with two beasts of warders beside me and I was the one who was not allowed to touch *you*! Kept away from the man I love by iron bars!

MACLEAN: *[Not wanting to hear this.]* Ordinary people made sacrifices for our sake. Money was collected. You never went without food or shelter. There was always someone there to look after you.

AGNES: *[Enraged.]* It's *not enough*, Johnnie! *You* weren't there! *[She turns away at this.]*

MACLEAN: *[Taken aback at the passion.]* I can't give it up yet, Agnes. Not at this stage. It's going to happen here soon, on the Clyde. Sometimes what a person believes is more important than what other people think of him or want him to do.

AGNES: And *this* is more important to you than me and the girls?

MACLEAN: Agnes! Nearly half a million people lined the streets of Glasgow and cheered when they heard what happened in Russia. Nearly half a million! I can't let it go now. One hundred thousand people opposed Lloyd George and said that *I* should get the freedom of Glasgow. Not him.

AGNES: Can you not learn the lessons of history? The police and the army have had plenty of training in Ireland should they ever have to come to Glasgow to stop a revolution. Government spies are everywhere. There is a policeman watching the house just now.

MACLEAN: Agnes. They had to release me because of working-class pressure. And that's where I put my faith. Look at the telegram the Russian workers sent. *[Holds it up and reads it.]* "Greetings are sent to the brave fighter for the International, Comrade Maclean, and we have hope that the new rise of international solidarity will bring him liberty".

AGNES: Can you not just accept a salaried job and stick to it?

MACLEAN: *[Seeing a way out.]* I might be able to get work with the Scottish Labour College, Agnes. The classes in economics are starting again this winter. That will give us regular money.

AGNES: *[Beginning to waver.]* Will you make sure you don't do anything silly?

MACLEAN: Of course I won't. There are over five hundred pupils who have enrolled for evening classes so far. I wouldn't want to let them down, would I?

AGNES: *[Pressing.]* Or me?

MACLEAN: *[Agreeing.]* Or you.

[Agnes accepts this resolutely and continues setting the table. Maclean resumes reading. The silence continues.]

***

SCENE IV

[The winter of 1917-1918. Two maintenance engineers in a munitions factory in Glasgow are having a smoke-break in a specially-designated room. Sounds of production line machinery are in the background. The men are working overtime on a mid-week evening. They are dressed in

navy-blue overalls and smoke throughout the duration of this conversation. The tone is easy and relaxed, the conversation of two acquaintances passing the time.]

JAMES: *[Lighting Gavin's cigarette.]* How many hours have you put in this week?

GAVIN: *[Leaning back, puffing smoke.]* Saturday morning, all day Sunday, three hours Monday night, tonight's Wednesday. Time and a half Saturday, double time Sunday, time and a half Monday and Wednesday. Thirty one hours. Good money.

JAMES: I'm the same. It's been like this every week for months now. You might as well take advantage of the overtime while you're getting it. It won't last for ever.

GAVIN: What makes you say that? What reason is there for the work to stop? There will always be war.

JAMES: I'm not so sure. I was coming out of the game last Saturday and I heard some of those Socialists, you know, the ones who hang around till the crowds appear, saying that the War was nearly over and that we should end it right away.

GAVIN: I don't think that will happen.

JAMES: Why not?

GAVIN: McKelvie in Production said to the gaffer that once Britain and Germany stop fighting they'll turn on Russia. That would mean more munitions, more machines breaking down, more work for us.

[They smoke in silence for a while.]

JAMES: Have you thought about what would happen if the War ended?

GAVIN: We've talked about it, the wife and me. There's plenty of work in America. I've got a brother out there just now. William.

JAMES: What's he doing?

GAVIN: Working with Ford motor cars. He says they can make a complete car from scratch in three and a half hours. Fantastic!

JAMES: I don't believe that.

GAVIN: *[Defensive.]* It's true. They use film cameras to watch the cars being made then there's a group of them go and examine the films and see how they can speed up production of any bit that's slower than the rest.

JAMES: You saying that they assemble the parts, screw the bits up and paint the thing in three and a half hours?

GAVIN: *[Decisive.]* Three and a half hours. The lot.

JAMES: *[Thinking seriously.]* You fancy that kind of work?

GAVIN: *[Blowing out smoke.]* We've talked about emigrating. William's been there for two years. He's bought his own house and he says he's going to buy his own car next year. And he was working in here as a fitter three years ago, very same as you and me, same apprenticeship, same money. Look at him now.

JAMES: House and a car?

GAVIN: House and a car.

JAMES: That's a lot for a working man, isn't it?

GAVIN: The hours are long but the money's good. There's no way he would come back here now. There's work in South Africa as well.

Hundreds of vacancies if you've got a trade. Good contacts through the Craft.

JAMES: A man up our close went there. I was talking to his mother on Saturday night. She said he's got his own servants.

GAVIN: Servants?

JAMES: The blacks there can't get a job for a white man. They'll do any kind of work for any money. Just like slaves. They do all the dirty work. Cleaning, gardening. The whites have all got gardens.

GAVIN: I could get used to that.

JAMES: In his garden there are fruit trees, oranges and apples and all that stuff. He makes even more money when it comes to harvest time. He sells it to the canning factory near where he lives, some Dutch firm. All the white workers do it. He's no different from the rest.

GAVIN: That sounds the life. It might be easier for me to get into America through the brother. Live with him till we get a place of our own.

JAMES: It seems as if there are plenty of Scottish guys out there. Might be worth thinking about.

GAVIN: *[Finishing cigarette.]* You're maybe right.

JAMES: *[Stubbing his cigarette out on the floor.]* Let's get back. Givven will be looking for us. Not long to go now. This is easy money when you can get it.

[They laugh and exeunt together, hands in pockets of their boiler suits.]

***

SCENE V

[Late May 1918. Maclean has been imprisoned for the second time. In a bar in the House of Commons following a debate on the new Food Rationing Bill Sir Auckland Geddes, Sir George Cave and Winston Churchill are discussing the general political situation. They move with their drinks from the bar area to a table facing the audience.]

CHURCHILL: *[With authority.]* Sit here, men. This will do.

[They settle into chairs.]

GEDDES: *[Generally.]* You think the War will end soon?

CAVE: Of course. Can't go on much longer. Now the Americans are in and the damned Soviets out. Eh, Winston?

CHURCHILL: *[Puffing cigar.]* Give it six months at the most. The German government is now shooting its own soldiers and sailors. They're involved in mutiny for more food and an end to the fighting in the trenches. The Germans won't be able to stand that kind of pressure for much longer.

GEDDES: *[Concerned.]* I've been a bit worried myself about the news here. They say there's talk of a revolution on the Clyde.

[The other two laugh patronisingly.]

CAVE: A revolution in Britain, Geddes? Not likely.

GEDDES: I'm not so sure. Lloyd George sent me up there. He wanted me to try and stop the strikes in the factories. I got nowhere. I spoke briefly and they were very hostile. I've never seen so many hostile to our way of life. They want something different. They want a revolution. The problem is that so many of them are educated. Not in our way, but you know what I mean. They know the political and economic arguments.

[The other two make it clear that they do not take him seriously.]

CHURCHILL: *[Mocking.]* Educated, eh? Peasants from the bogs? They're no threat to us. *[Puffs on his cigar then more seriously.]* It's the damned Soviets we should be worried about.

CAVE: *[Agreeing with Churchill.]* We'll have to watch Ireland too. When the War ends we should be able to transfer a good number of our troops over to Dublin. Let them get rid of their anger over there on the Sinn Fein people.

GEDDES: *[Still mildly protesting.]* We should keep some troops ready to go up to Glasgow. Not Jock regiments. Apparently this Maclean fellow has been made Russian Consul in Britain, whatever that's supposed to mean. Although he's in contact with Lenin and Trotsky, so our people say. *[They smoke and drink in silence for a while.]*

CHURCHILL: *[Thoughtfully.]* Maclean is in prison, is he not? What can he do to hurt us?

GEDDES: *[Triumphant.]* Yes, he is just now. But he'll be out some time, maybe soon if the authorities are pressurised the way they were the last time Maclean was in prison. They were talking of a general strike and taking over the means of production when I was there. They mean it too. Occupying the food stores, seizing the farms, taking over the Post Offices and the City administration. Just like Ireland.

CAVE: Who would run the show?

GEDDES: Workers' Committees.

CHURCHILL: *[Snorting with contempt.]* Workers' Committees! You really are taking it too far, Geddes. This is ridiculous. Those kind of people can't even run their own lives, never mind others'. *[Puffs]* I'm afraid I can't go along with that.

GEDDES: The Russians have already appointed Maclean.

CHURCHILL: They can appoint who they like. That's of no concern to us. We have refused to recognise the Soviet Government in Petrograd therefore, de facto, we refuse to recognise Maclean.

GEDDES: We can't do that! The people adore him. On May Day there were hundreds of thousands out on the streets shouting his name, calling for his release.

CHURCHILL: Tell him George.

CAVE: First we ban public meetings of any kind. More than two people together and we read the Riot Act. We forbid publication of any printed matter unless it passes our censorship test in the Press Bureau. We forbid the let of all public halls, of whatever size, for public meetings of any kind. That will do.

GEDDES: *[Doubtful in the face of this catalogue of evidence.]* I'm not sure. What about the money Maclean is getting from Russia?

CHURCHILL: *[Dismissively.]* Any letters we will stop and examine. Hold them a few weeks then send them back to the sender. We've been doing that in Ireland for a while. Seize any money sent to Maclean and get the bankers to refuse to accept his signature on cheques. It's not difficult, Geddes.

GEDDES: They say that once he's out he'll be going to Russia to see it all for himself. See how it runs in practice so that he can bring back a working model.

CAVE: *[Calmly.]* Refuse him a visa to travel. If he goes illegally, arrest him for that.

GEDDES: *[Losing.]* What about the general strike! The very mention of his name is enough to get thousands of them out on the streets.

CAVE: Initiate Workers' Councils or something like that. A few token *representatives* to defuse the situation. Give them a taste of the good life, the usual things. They go back and argue our case for us and we get the press to say it's all in the workers' interests.

[Cave and Churchill laugh together.]

CHURCHILL: Get the press to say he's a bad boy then throw in something about his mental state. That's always a good one. What's he in for anyway?

GEDDES: Sedition and causing mutiny.

CHURCHILL: Good. Next time that will help put him away for a lot longer. The mob is fickle. Remember Coriolanus.

CAVE: Most of the other Reds can't stand him anyway. Hyndman and his people. We deported Maclean's secretary to Russia. We'll see how he gets on in his workers' Heaven!

GEDDES: I still think there will be some kind of trouble up there, something will happen.

CHURCHILL: Stop worrying, Geddes. We're holding back food supplies to Glasgow to starve them into accepting rationing. It's all under control. *We* have got the guns and *we* have got the tanks. Marvellous things.

CAVE: With Maclean drugged in prison and the peasants drugged outside we have nothing to worry about.

CHURCHILL: *[Indicates for service.]* Three brandies. I say, what *about* Ireland?

[Lights fade against the sound of conversation and drinks being served.]

ACT FOUR

SCENE I

[Autumn 1919. Maclean by now is thin, white and haggard. He has the gaunt look of a man who has been on hunger strike and has been force-fed. He is walking to a seat with Ruaraidh Erskine, the Honourable Stuart Erskine of Mar, a leading Scottish Nationalist, at the top of Queen's Park overlooking Glasgow. They are enjoying the crisp air and the view over the city.]

ERSKINE: *[As they sit.]* It's good to be able to see Ben Lomond so clearly. *[After a pause.]* What work do you think you'll do now?

MACLEAN: *[Tired.]* Now that the School Board has refused to reinstate me as a teacher? *[He looks round and speaks in a detached way.]* Continue my work for what I believe in. The revolution.

ERSKINE: Money?

MACLEAN: Voluntary contributions. The workers always give to their own. Some days are better than others.

ERSKINE: And Agnes?

MACLEAN: *[Reluctant.]* She's always supported me in the past. *[There is an underlying tension.]*

ERSKINE: So you can't answer me one way or the other?

MACLEAN: *[Wearily.]* I can't see the Scottish Home Rule movement doing anything. Too many divisions.

ERSKINE: We need people like you if there's to be any chance at all. Maxton and the others have pledged their word. *[Enthusiastic.]* We're hoping to model ourselves on the Irish.

MACLEAN: *[Seeing the vision but caught.]* A marvellous achievement. But I don't know. One half of Scotland doesn't know what the other half is doing. We're still divided by class.

ERSKINE: But if you came in with us…

MACLEAN: The Irish followed the Sinn Feiners, not Irish Labour.

ERSKINE: John, that doesn't matter! The Irish have their own parliament! You've said it often enough, John. Scotland and England are different.

MACLEAN: It could become just like America and Mexico. The workers get turned against each other. And in fifty years the Americans become so much more powerful.

ERSKINE: John. Scotland is like a priceless piece of stained glass without a lead frame to support it. We are going to have to fight to support it ourselves.

MACLEAN: The establishment won't accept it, Ruaraidh. Look what happened to Shinwell and the others when the general strike failed. I know what it's like. I've suffered at the hands of those people. I've *had* a rubber tube forced up my nose and down my throat.

ERSKINE: We won't even be represented as a nation at the Peace Conference yet there are Scottish corpses lying in France. I'm tired of my people being treated as expendable by the military.

MACLEAN: I accept the need for Scotland to run its own affairs. Taxes, the military, everything. But what do my people have in common with the landowners? Look at the history of this country. When has someone in power ever done anything for the peasants?

ERSKINE: But I believe in co-operative working and wealth being shared co-operatively too.

[There is a moment's silence as Maclean thinks about this.]

MACLEAN: You do?

ERSKINE: And Gallacher and Kirkwood have promised their support for me. You think about it John. Celtic Communism. I'll contact you in a month for an article.

[They begin to walk away, off stage.]

MACLEAN: Labour Party are traitors you reckon?

ERSKINE: Every last one of them, John. Bought by London gold.

[Exeunt.]

***

SCENE II

[Autumn 1919. Night time. The living room of Maclean's house as before. Agnes has a suitcase open on the table. She is busy going to and fro, packing various things she needs. She looks haggard and drawn as if she has suffered greatly. She is much more quiet and determined now, no longer arguing with Maclean in an emotional way. Maclean enters, clutching pamphlets, having just returned from a political meeting. He stands and watches her in silence for a moment.]

MACLEAN: *[Obviously disturbed.]* What's wrong? What are you doing?

AGNES: *[Quiet and calm.]* I'm leaving, John. *[She continues to pack.]*

MACLEAN: *[Shocked, sits down.]* What do you mean?

AGNES: I'm leaving you and the house. I can't take any more.

MACLEAN: *[Looking round.]* What about Nan and Jean? Where are they? In bed?

AGNES: No, they're away already. Rose came this morning to take them down to Elizabeth's. I've told them we're going on a holiday.

MACLEAN: Why now, Agnes? I need you to be here with me.

AGNES: *[Stops, looks at him.]* No, you don't, John. You don't, and that's the problem. I've asked you a thousand times, pleaded with you to give up some of the political work so that we could have time together to ourselves and every time you have ignored me. You keep saying there's so much to do and so little time to do it in and so few people to help with the cause. Well, now I'm tired hearing that. It's not me you need or want, John, it's just someone who can run a free hotel for your revolutionary friends.

[There is silence between them for a moment as they absorb this.]

MACLEAN: *[Suspicious.]* Is someone getting at you? *[Becoming angry.]* Have the police been around here again scaring you about me going back to prison? *[Beginning to shout.]* Have they?

AGNES: *[Quietly.]* No, John. Nobody's been near me.

MACLEAN: Don't lie to me!

AGNES: *[Directly.]* I'm not lying to you, John. I've supported you all these years. All those nights waiting for you to come in from endless meetings, all those nights when you were in prison and I went alone to a cold bed after seeing to the house and the children, all that time which should have been our married life together gone, and we'll never be able to retrieve it.

MACLEAN: I haven't changed from the day we met!

AGNES: Maybe it's me, John. I've sacrificed a lot of things but the greatest sacrifice of all has been my husband. Look at yourself in the mirror, John. You're forty years of age and you should be in your prime, enjoying your wife and your young girls. Look at you. You're dying on your feet. Your biggest revolutionary act would be to give up politics.

MACLEAN: But I've got to take advantage of the situation in Scotland at the moment!

AGNES: *[Calm.]* I am not listening any more, John. All I hear about is petty in-fighting. You've been sacked. That's not very revolutionary, is it? You have neglected your family. Until you start putting us first, I'm going to keep the kids down in the country. It won't make any difference, they never see you from one day to the next as it is.

MACLEAN: *[Quickly.]* I could re-apply to get into teaching.

AGNES: *[Finishing packing.]* You do that, John. You re-apply. Once you've started again as a full-time salaried teacher and once you're ready to say that three nights of the week and one day at the weekend are for your wife and family and nobody else then I'll bring the kids back. But not until. *[She closes the suitcase and begins tightening the straps.]*

MACLEAN: *[Changing the subject irrationally.]* There's never been another woman, Agnes.

AGNES: *[Laughs sardonically.]* No-one else would be daft enough to put up with you. You're so shabby the wee one is ashamed to be seen outside the door with you.

MACLEAN: *[Hurt at this.]* Who? Nan?

AGNES: *[Lifts the case onto the floor.]* Yes. All the other kids call her daddy a tramp and she's been home in tears more than once. But of course you're never here to know about that. Well, John, I'll away.

MACLEAN: *[Tired.]* What about money?

AGNES: We'll manage for the time being. Rose has arranged a small cottage for us next door to her and she says some of the big houses take on cleaners and the like at this time of year. I might manage to get a start that way.

MACLEAN: Working for the masters! What about your pleurisy?

AGNES: *[Detached.]* It hasn't concerned you before, John, you've no need to worry about it at this stage. *[She picks up the suitcase.]* Well, I'll have to go. I'm catching the last train. I promised I would tuck the wee ones into bed. *[She moves towards him to kiss him.]* I hope I hear from you sooner rather than later. I'll get the children to write to you. *[She bends down and kisses him lightly then leaves without looking back.]*

MACLEAN: *[Sits in the chair for a time then rises and looks to the door.]* Agnes! *[He stops, puts his hands in his coat pockets. He sees a cup lying on the table. He picks this up and hurls it at the wall where it smashes. He returns to a chair and sits down. The lights fade on him into darkness.]*

***

SCENE III

[Easter 1920. London. A pre-conference committee meeting of the British Socialist Party. Theodore Rothstein, chief Bolshevik representative in Britain, is in the chair. Lieutenant Colonel Malone M.P., leader of the British Socialist Party, is present as are two executive members, Inkpin and Cant. Maclean is having to defend accusations he has made. There is a tense silence in the room.]

ROTHSTEIN: Comrades, we come to the main business of the evening. Some of the accusations Comrade Maclean has been making against Comrade Malone are very serious ones, given that Comrade Malone is the leader of the British Socialist Party. We would like these matters cleared up before our annual conference tomorrow.

MALONE: Thank you, Comrade Rothstein. My motion, seconded by Comrade Rothstein, reads as follows. *[He refers to his notes.]* "That Comrade John Maclean, in the light of his recent anti-working class statements and actions, be expelled from the British Socialist Party." *[He looks round.]* Comrade Maclean seems to think we have been corrupted by ill-gotten money. I would like to hear Comrade Maclean's response in the interests of fairness, justice and democracy.

[There is another tense pause while Maclean looks at the face of each man in turn before he speaks.]

MACLEAN: *[Calmly referring to his notes when necessary.]* I am reluctant to call you 'Comrades' any more. Malone's accusations deserve contempt rather than a reasonable reply. Between March and April last year I spoke at Lanark, Hamilton, Colne, Nelson, Burnley, Glasgow, Sheffield, Paisley, Carlisle and Cardiff. No person on this committee has helped me in any way in my campaign. However, that does not matter now. I would rather be judged by people of my own class than by people like you. Malone has always been anti-Soviet, acting as if he is a Government spy. I make no apologies to people like you for putting forward my beliefs. Socialism means that you are free and are free to speak. *[He pauses to look round again.]* I want to know if the finances for this Party are coming from the money and jewels currently being smuggled out of Russia. I refuse to be a paid lackey of Lenin. I must be free to criticise what I think has gone wrong with the Revolution in Russia. If we are not being financed by Russia, then the money must be coming from the British Government. That would mean that Malone is a Government agent. In any case, I will be returning to Scotland to pursue with increased vigour the establishment of a Scottish Workers' Republic. I want nothing to do with a tinkering reform of

Capitalism. That really is all I have to say to you gentlemen.

ROTHSTEIN: *[Slightly embarrassed.]* Well, would any Comrade like to contribute to the debate in any way?

[There is silence.]

Well, Comrade Malone, all that remains really for you to do is sum up your own response.

MALONE: *[With a show of anger.]* Maclean's comments have only served to confirm my belief that he no longer has any meaningful part to play in the great Socialist movement. I utterly repudiate the slanderous statements of a man who is clearly mentally unwell. I would seek the support of my Comrades in this resolution. That is all I have to say in reply.

ROTHSTEIN: No further contributions?

[Again there is silence.]

Well, that means we should now proceed to the vote. All those in favour of Comrade Malone's resolution please show.

[Rothstein, Malone, Inkpin and Cant indicate.]

All those against?

[Maclean refuses to vote.]

I hereby declare Comrade John Maclean expelled from the British Socialist Party and no longer able to take part in any of its business.

[Maclean rises and leaves. The others follow him with their eyes. There is a continuing silence.]

MALONE: *[Trying to laugh.]* He's mad, you know. Obsessed. Even people like Gallacher are saying he's gone completely off his head. His wife has left him too. Pressure of work. Persecution mania they call it. Next business?

ROTHSTEIN: *[Briskly.]* Next business. *[He reads.]* "That a General Strike would not be in the best interests of International Socialism if the Allies cross the Rhine."

[The lights fade.]

***

SCENE IV

[May 1920. The isolation ward of a mental hospital near Glasgow. James MacDougall is sitting in a chair looking out of the window onto a full spring morning. He is on his own for his safety and the safety of others. He is recovering from a nervous breakdown but although his speech is sluggish his mind is lucid and associative. Maclean enters, formally dressed in a coat, hat and three-piece suit. He is obviously distressed at having to see his close friend in such circumstances.]

MACLEAN: *[Heartily.]* James! How are you doing?

[MacDougall looks at him carefully but does not answer. Maclean becomes uneasy.]

I thought I would come up and see you. I heard you were due to get out soon!

MACDOUGALL: *[Slowly, as if drugged.]* John Maclean. What do you want?

MACLEAN: *[Trying to laugh off this welcome.]* I went to see your mother last week. She said you were doing really well and would be out soon. I thought we could make some plans. I miss working with you.

MACDOUGALL: *[Singing in flat tone.]*
'Little man, little man,
You want to be a soldier little man,
You are mother's only son –
Never mind about the gun,
Stay at home,
Fight for her
All you can.'

MACLEAN: *[Uneasily.]* I had forgotten that one, Jimmy. It seems like a different age altogether.

MACDOUGALL: *[Looking out of the window.]* A different age? It's just the same as it always was, as it always will be. My father was a Tory.

MACLEAN: *[Looking at the floor.]* You worked harder than any of us. You deserve this rest.

MACDOUGALL: *[Scornful.]* Rest! Don't patronise me, Johnnie! They've had me strapped on a bed in the quiet room. Have you ever felt what it's like not to be able to move at all, not even a finger? I'm mad and I'm broken. I'm not resting. And the others in here have been with the rats in the trenches.

MACLEAN: *[Knowing he cannot deceive MacDougall by being jolly.]* I'm sorry, Jimmy, I really am. I never expected this. *[He takes his hat off and looks at it.]* I never realised how important you were to me until you were no longer there.

MACDOUGALL: *[Taunting.]* Selfish John Maclean! *You* didn't realise! What about me? I didn't realise my life was pouring onto the streets.

MACLEAN: *[Hardening.]* These sacrifices have to be made. *[He pauses.]* Agnes has left me.

MACDOUGALL: Agnes. You won your bride from the borders. The Young Lochinvar has come out of the West. His steed was the best. Have you gone and lost your bride?

MACLEAN: *[Changing the subject.]* I'm going to Russia soon. I've made my application.

MACDOUGALL: The Union of Soviet Socialist Republics. God Save The King! They still sing that at night. They think the Germans are bad people. Not made bad. *[In a moment of intensity.]* Johnnie, why are people mad?

MACLEAN: *[Hoping for some connection.]* I don't know. What do you think?

MACDOUGALL: I could never speak in public. I hated it. I wanted to keep working. I have watched the snowdrops working this winter. They worked harder this year than I ever did. I had never really thought about them before. The attendants had heard of me before I came in. The great speaker who worked with John Maclean. They are kind to me. They bind me.

MACLEAN: *[Changing the subject again.]* They say the revolution in Russia's going to be successful. There's work and food for everyone. They're building decent houses for all the people. They're taking peasants and making them into scientists. There's ballet and opera for ordinary working people. And books! It's got to come here!

MACDOUGALL: What's Red John Maclean's friend doing in a place like this? I can see them sniggering. Scotland. Frightened to rule itself. Hirpling along behind Europe's tumbrils. The tartan prostitute of the Empire.

[There is a pause while Maclean thinks of a reply.]

MACLEAN: Are you all right for food? I can arrange for anything you want to be brought in.

MACDOUGALL: *[Mock outrage.]* What, and be better than everyone else who's in here? I watch the squirrels eating and I eat the food. And I watch the men in here holding their heads tightly. Feet rotted in the mud. Some wanted to be friends with the Germans.

MACLEAN: I was told the officers shot their own who wanted to unite.

MACDOUGALL: They've got new machines for men with no legs. Women walk the streets in Germany. Soldiers have money and women walk the streets. All the artists say we can't have art after a war like that. No more war.

MACLEAN: *[Seeing he is getting nowhere.]* Look, Jimmy, I'll have to go just now. *[Awkward.]* I'll come back again before you're out. I'll let you know how everyone in the movement is getting on.

MACDOUGALL: *[Sitting, watching.]* You won't be back, Johnnie. They don't like it here, with the smell of bodies and disinfectant. Everything's clean in a mad house.

MACLEAN: *[Tense with the discomfort.]* Take care of yourself, Jimmy. I'll see you next week. *[He holds out his hand.]*

[MacDougall refuses to shake Maclean's hand. Maclean withdraws his, shuffles nervously and makes to leave. MacDougall turns his face away from him.]

***

SCENE V

[May 1920. An office in the House of Lords. Lord Curzon, Foreign Secretary, is going through mail with his Permanent Secretary. They are

seated at a table facing the audience. They sift desultorily through a pile of envelopes.]

CURZON: *[Wearily.]* I think the main focus should be on rebuilding links with Germany. Are there any more with a German postmark?

SECRETARY: *[Going through a few more.]* No, I think that's the last one, Lord Curzon. The private visit next month to discuss trade contacts has just been confirmed. There's a huge market because of all the reconstruction needed. It could help us find alternative employment for the returning soldiers and the redundant munitions workers.

CURZON: *[Reflectively.]* Yes, the great unwashed. Home Secretary is worried about the prospect of mass unemployment. Civil unrest and all that. Political agitation. And the worry of putting troops in against the Socialists. They might not want to fight their own kind.

SECRETARY: Will we continue to pay the soldiers a higher-than-average wage?

CURZON: That's the general intention. Police and army. Buy loyalty. What else is there?

SECRETARY: *[Passes over an envelope.]* There's this here from John Maclean, the Scotch revolutionary.

CURZON: I thought he was in prison. No, he's out, that's right. What does he want? Just read it to me.

SECRETARY: *[Takes envelope back, takes out letter and begins to read.]*
'Lord Curzon,
I am hereby requesting permission to visit Russia during the months of July and August 1920 when the Second Congress of the Third International is due to take place.
Yours etc.,

John MacLean.'
[He pauses and looks over at Lord Curzon.]

CURZON: He is one worth watching, but we'll get him in the end through his own folly. He's now in this Communist Party which has been set up. Yes, he is a potentially dangerous man. What do you think?

SECRETARY: It seems to me there are two courses of action open to us. Either a straightforward refusal on a pretext we can easily arrange or… *[He pauses.]*

CURZON: *[Leaning forward, more interested.]* Or what?

SECRETARY: *[Matter-of-fact tone.]* Or we let him go abroad and we have him killed while he is on the Continent. That would be fairly easy. *[He looks back at the letter.]*

CURZON: *[Thinks deeply.]* Yes, that's a possibility. *[There is a moment's silence while they consider this.]* We could keep stalling until it's too late for him to make arrangements then give him permission?

SECRETARY: He might try to go illegally. Through Denmark and Sweden. Out of England through Leith. They say he is very popular there.

CURZON: No, he's stupid enough to be open and honest in the way he goes about things. I am assuming there will be a police spy watching his movements. Then there are our own people in the Socialist movements. *[Assured.]* No, he won't go illegally.

SECRETARY: He attracts large crowds.

CURZON: Large, but peaceful. The Government worries only when the rabble starts to riot. *[He laughs lightly.]*

SECRETARY: How would you like me to reply?

CURZON: Let me see. Something like this. *[The Secretary takes notes as Lord Curzon speaks.]* 'Lord Curzon is unable to give you a reply to your request at this moment, but if you will apply to him again towards the end of next month he will consider whether the necessary facilities can be granted to you or not.' *[He pauses while the Secretary scribbles.]* We can do that a couple of times then take it from there. Refer to the instability of the international situation. Do you agree?

SECRETARY: Yes, that seems to be the best way. Go quietly at first.

CURZON: What else is there?

SECRETARY: A request from the South African Government for you to go on a fact-finding tour and bring as many of the press with you as possible. All expenses paid.

CURZON: *[Stifling a yawn.]* Too much port last night. Why do they want that?

SECRETARY: They say there's a great need for white, skilled workers and they would like to attract soldiers back from the war to go there. They are looking for sympathetic coverage.

CURZON: *[Interested.]* Can we fit it in?

SECRETARY: *[Eagerly.]* Yes, we *can,* as a matter of fact. The month after next, when we return from Germany. It will be a pleasant sail in the sunshine.

CURZON: Will we be able to persuade the others?

SECRETARY: With the prospect of mass unemployment?

CURZON: *[Decisively.]* Start to make the arrangements. I'll swing it with the P.M. I'm bored with these tiresome domestic squabbles. There must be more to life than this.

SECRETARY: *[Smiling and writing at the same time.]* I'll make this one a priority, Sir!

[The lights fade on them.]

END OF ACT FOUR

***

ACT FIVE

SCENE I

[August 1920. The kitchen of Gress croft on the Hebridean Island of Lewis. Maclean is sitting with two raiders, crofters who have seized their own land and are trying to resist forced eviction by Lord Leverhume, the soap magnate. They have just finished a meal. The raiders are dressed in blue calico trousers and jackets. It is a perfectly still summer's evening.]

1ST RAIDER: We had only heard of you by name before, but your father and grandfather are remembered by fishermen on Mull.

2ND RAIDER: And spoken well of too.

MACLEAN: *[Pleased.]* The air is wonderful. I was glad of the sail over, although I had to share the deck with milk from Aberdeen and sheep bound for the cleared land.

2ND RAIDER: *[With slow anger.]* We can't live on fresh air and scenery. It's very hard for the people here just now.

MACLEAN: Why were they bringing milk that kind of distance?

1ST RAIDER: They're bringing it here by the gallon to break the spirit of the people. Leverhulme says he has to clear us off our crofts as part of his big dairy farming scheme to supply milk to Stornoway. It's not true.

MACLEAN: *[Recognising the point.]* True. If milk can be brought in now then it can be brought in afterwards. When the people of Lewis have been forced into Stornoway to work for him.

1ST RAIDER: When the crofts are dead he will open his canning factory and the people will have to work for him because there will be no other way to make a living.

2ND RAIDER: Our way of life will go. After all the sacrifices we made in the war. I don't want to spend *my* life locked up working His Lordship's hours and neither do any of the others.

MACLEAN: *[Intense.]* This canning factory. Tell me more about it. Some of the Clyde Workers' Committee are saying it's the start of the western seaboard becoming a line of military installations.

1ST RAIDER: Leverhulme wants the land cleared. Then the Mac Line trawlers will sail to Iceland and Greenland for fish which will be processed in his factory. That would be a good cover for the Navy and would make him plenty of money.

2ND RAIDER: The big boats will force out the local fleet because they will pay higher wages at first. Then there won't be a local boat left. The fishing industry in this country could go for ever.

MACLEAN: Can the boats fish the deep waters just now?

1ST RAIDER: Just in the good weather they can go into the very deep stretches. But that's only two months in the year. The big trawlers would be able to go out all year round to keep the factory running.

MACLEAN: *[Sardonically.]* Or he could put the factory workers on short time. You have to resist this now.

1ST RAIDER: The people here will take too much on trust, John. They always have done, listening to the lairds and the ministers, going off and fighting imperialist wars.

MACLEAN: They'll have men in the Navy like these deep-sea fishermen who will know the waters well in all weathers. That would be handy in the event of a war with America!

2ND RAIDER: *[Genuinely puzzled at this mental leap.]* War with America? I'm afraid I don't follow you there, John.

MACLEAN: *[Sweeps his arm in a slow curve.]* America won't sit back and watch Britain control the North Atlantic passages. Stornoway to the Faroes to Iceland and on to Greenland and Canada. They will soon start to squabble about overseas markets.

[They reflect on this new picture being suggested.]

1ST RAIDER: I don't know if we can hold fast, John. The people are under pressure to sell the crofts and farms.

2ND RAIDER: There's even talk of prisons. The people here know nothing of prisons. We don't have such a thing. We don't even have a policeman here.

1ST RAIDER: Leverhulme has stopped work on roads and harbours to force people into hardship. Money is changing hands. The factors of the Duke of Sutherland and the Marquis of Graham are telling people they would be better off if they moved soon. There are subsidies to go to Canada and New Zealand. The people will follow the land.

MACLEAN: It makes my blood boil. All that Scottish land lying idle too, our own land. Our land. Our fish. *[He quietens.]*

[There is another pause while they reflect on this.]

1ST RAIDER: You need to know the winters here, John. It's hard scraping a living, hard to keep body and soul together. Any regular paid work would be better for the people, Scotland or no Scotland. *[Pauses.]* And anyway, our Scotland might be different from the one you know. You'll find out soon enough tonight.

MACLEAN: It's all there, land and wealth and people. We don't want a parish council! We need complete independence. And it will come, just as sure as it is coming in Egypt and India and Africa and Ireland!

2ND RAIDER: We'll go now, John. The rest of the crofters will be waiting to hear what you have to say. I wish you luck.

[Exeunt all three, putting on jackets and caps.]

***

SCENE II

[25th October 1921. The High Court in Glasgow with Sheriff Boyd presiding. Maclean is in the dock conducting his own defence. It is towards the end of the trial.]

BOYD: *[To the jury.]* The eleven counts of the indictment have been read and you have heard the evidence of the Chief Constable. *[He pauses and speaks directly but unsympathetically to Maclean.]* How do you plead to the eleven points of the charge that you "addressed an audience of the civilian population and used language calculated as likely to cause sedition and disaffection among His Majesty's Forces and among the civilian population"?

MACLEAN: *[Clearly.]* Not guilty on all counts! Whatever I said was in my own words and not as reported in this court by various senior police officers. I have always argued that workers should not confine themselves to industrial action but should take political action as well. I am working for a Scottish Workers' Republic. I said we would not use violence; violence would be used first against us. After the War came the usual economic collapse. And the only big city in which the unemployed are organised, where no riots have taken place, is Glasgow.

BOYD: *[Intervening.]* You have omitted to mention one vital point. According to the evidence against you, you said at a public meeting, "Take food if you are hungry". It is crucial that we establish whether or not this was said by you.

MACLEAN: I said – and I was careful to say it – "There is plenty of food in the country and round about – don't starve!"

BOYD: *[Pressing again.]* A further point not clearly explained is who exactly finances your operations?

MACLEAN: I am a tutor at the Scottish Labour College, and you already know that.

BOYD: How did you come to organise the unemployed, then?

MACLEAN: Because nobody else would.

BOYD: How many follow your banner?

MACLEAN: I do not know that, but I do know there are millions without work.

BOYD: Why did you lead those unemployed people to the churches?

MACLEAN: To let the church people see at first hand those who were starving.

BOYD: What about the Cathedral and the Infirmary?

MACLEAN: I led the unemployed up to the Cathedral to get shelter there for those who were lying out in George Square and elsewhere.

BOYD: *[Interrupting.]* Before you go any further I would like to point out to the jury that question by question you are condemning yourself. However, please finish.

MACLEAN: I will fight against the tyranny of Capitalism until it kills me or until I die naturally. I object to this form of society where a few people own the world and the rest form a wage-slave class. For my views I have been dismissed as a school teacher and have been sentenced to five years penal servitude. I have chosen to exercise my democratic right to speak and the forces of the state have been used to silence me. And I say to you that I am glad of this trial today because it has brought out at last that John Maclean is not prepared to see human beings die of starvation. *[Maclean sits.]*

BOYD: *[Dryly.]* A grand finale but not enough to save you. *[To the jury.]* I direct you to find this man guilty on all eleven indicted counts and leave you to determine the length of the sentence. *[He bangs the gavel.]* Clear the courtroom for one hour.

[Maclean is led away to the cells while the jury members debate amongst themselves.]

***

SCENE III

[October 1922. Barlinnie Prison, Glasgow, the day prior to Maclean's release. He has served his full term. Maclean is walking in a circle and talking with the Reverend William Fulton, assistant prison chaplain. Maclean is physically very frail, white-haired and looking much older than his forty three years. His passion is still in evidence, but the time in prison has taken its toll. As a political prisoner he is in civilian clothes. A warder is present at the start of the conversation.]

FULTON: That's all right, officer, you can go.

OFFICER: Sir! *[Exit.]*

FULTON: You must find them incredibly ignorant, John, a man of your intelligence.

MACLEAN: Not them all, William. But a few really do try my belief in human nature. Some of them boast to their friends that they are responsible for looking after John Maclean. That I find difficult to grasp.

FULTON: Have you been ill-treated recently?

MACLEAN: No, not this time. But some of the other prisoners take terrible beatings. You can hear them in the night. That depresses me, and I think of my own family then.

FULTON: *[Quietly.]* How are things with your wife? Is she coming tomorrow to meet you?

MACLEAN: I'm frightened I've lost her and the two wee ones for ever. In my life I had to make choices. *[Pauses.]* I would do it all again this way if I had to.

FULTON: Will the Labour College take you on as a lecturer?

MACLEAN: I'm not sure. Money at meetings has gone down. It's hard for the unemployed to pay to support me. But I'll work for nothing if need be.

FULTON: You would make a good Quaker, John!

MACLEAN: Hardly a Quaker! Those people were very brave. Maybe the Church of Scotland could learn from them and get rid of its land and property!

FULTON: *[Laughs lightly.]* We're not that bad, John! I know there's a few settle for christenings and weddings and funerals in leafy areas but there's still a lot of good work being done.

MACLEAN: Not in the places I see. How can a Church support war?

FULTON: You're too harsh, John. We give a lot of comfort to people of all classes.

MACLEAN: Ghost stories and fairy stories?

FULTON: Beautiful words of succour.

MACLEAN: I think Jesus was a Socialist who was bought and sold for money. And still is.

FULTON: Some of the men in here, even the hardened men, think that *you* are a kind of Jesus. I speak with them and I hear the respect they have for you. It's beyond money.

MACLEAN: *[Embarrassed.]* Not me, William. I couldn't mislead my own people.

[There is a lull in the conversation while they think about this.]

FULTON: I'm sure the teaching authorities will take you back.

MACLEAN: *[Bitter.]* That won't happen now. I think I'm banned sine die. Anyway, I don't want to waste any time when I get out. I'll be standing for the Unemployed Workers at the election in November.

FULTON: I hope you don't find yourself back in here, John. It's not good for you.

MACLEAN: I don't have long left. I have to try and fight for those who can't fight for themselves. Look at the case of Bernard Murdoch.

FULTON: *[Worried.]* Deaths in police custody are always a worry, John. All the chaplains share that concern. We do ask questions, you know, we don't just let it rest.

MACLEAN: Foul play is foul play! I'm working on a pamphlet called "The Glasgow Police Murder Hush-Up". I'm going to see that his wife gets a solicitor!

FULTON: *[With muted respect.]* That's not going to make the Glasgow Police better disposed towards you, John. They'll hound you for that.

MACLEAN: I'm not here on Earth to keep silent about injustice. I'll publish the names of those responsible.

FULTON: I wish I had your courage, John.

OFFICER: *[Returning.]* That's your time, Sir. The prisoner has to be returned to his cell now.

[Fulton and Maclean stop and look at each other.]

MACLEAN: Thank you for coming to see me, William. Despite my atheism, I recognise that you have supported me.

[They shake hands in a moment of emotional silence.]

FULTON: Take care outside, John. I know that when I'm an old man I'll be proud to say that I had these conversations with you. *[He holds Maclean's hands, closes his eyes and blesses him.]* "Let your light so shine before men, that they may see your good works, and glorify your Father which is in Heaven. Amen."

[Maclean is led out by the Officer. Fulton stands mid-stage, looking after him and thinking.]

***

SCENE IV

[Late November 1923. The interior of a room and kitchen in Glasgow. A mother is nursing a very sick child. Maclean enters, coughing. He is suffering from semi-starvation. He is poorly clad, thin and white, and speaks with difficulty because of his burst throat.]

MACLEAN: *[Hoarsely.]* I got your message, Mrs Shevlin. *[Coughs.]* I came as quickly as I could. *[Coughs.]* What's wrong with the wee one? *[He moves towards the cot.]*

MRS SHEVLIN: *[An edge of desperation in her voice.]* I couldn't think of anyone else to send for, Mr Maclean. I don't know what to do? Jamie's been sick for days now, and we don't have a lot of food left.

MACLEAN: *[Looks round the room.]* What about the fire? It's freezing damp in here. *[Coughs.]*

MRS SHEVLIN: *[Ashamed.]* We've no money at all, nothing. We've had no coal for a week now.

MACLEAN: *[Puts hand on her shoulder.]* Don't worry. You shouldn't have to be cold or hungry in this land. Here. Take this just now. *[Gives her some coins.]*

MRS SHEVLIN: *[Ashamed but consenting.]* Thank you, Mr Maclean. *[Pauses.]* I'll do what ever you want.

MACLEAN: When I leave, get a neighbour to buy coal. Then get some food and send for a doctor. There should be enough there to cover everything, even if the doctor charges more than you expect.

MRS SHEVLIN: I can't thank you enough. What about you? Are you all right yourself?

MACLEAN: *[Coughs.]* Aye. Think about the child. He's the future. I'll away. Now, do what I say and do it quickly. I'll be back in a few days to make sure you've got enough.

MRS SHEVLIN: *[Seeing him out.]* I don't know what to say to you. I didn't know what I was going to do.

MACLEAN: *[Self-effacing.]* Take care the now.

MRS SHEVLIN: Cheerio, Mr Maclean. And thanks again.

[The lights fade as she walks back to look at her child.]

SCENE V

[As before, in the editorial office of a London-based newspaper. The sub-editor is sitting at a table making occasional notes. The editor enters.]

EDITOR: Evening, David.

SUB: Evening, Sir. How are things? Enjoy dinner?

EDITOR: Marvellous. *[Looks over sub-editor's shoulder.]*

SUB: Just tidying up the loose ends. The front page is nearly there. *[Passes copy over.]*

EDITOR: *[Yawns and begins to skim read.]* "Hooliganism on the part of supporters of the Socialist cause continues to characterise local meetings. At one such gathering last night a Unionist candidate, Miss Violet Robertson, was the victim of a disgraceful attack. She was kicked violently by a member of the audience and had to be conveyed to her home in a motor car. This was despite the presence of a posse of constables and a number of C.I.D. men..." *[His voice tails off.]* Yes, that's quite good. *[He glances over the rest of the copy.]* Anything else?

SUB: Not a lot. There's this here. *[Picks up a sheet of paper.]* Maclean's obituary. I'm not sure where to put it. We don't have a lot of space tonight.

EDITOR: *[Glancing over the pages on the table.]* Stick it down the bottom of page twelve, beside that article on "Mendelism In Crop Breeding". *[He indicates with his finger.]*

SUB: I'll have to cut it quite a bit, then.

EDITOR: Doesn't matter. How does it read?

UB: There's a lot of local detail that will be fairly boring. *[Begins to ead.]* Mister John Maclean, prominent throughout the country as a man f extreme political views, died at his residence in Newlands, Glasgow, ıst night from an attack of pneumonia. A native of Glasgow, Mister Aaclean graduated in Arts at the University and for a number of years e was a teacher under the Govan School Board.

rom his college days he was a participant in fringe and Irish politics nd early in life he threw himself into the Labour movement. While in ıe past ten or twelve years he had played the part of a stormy petrel, abourists acknowledge the valuable propaganda work he did for the ause. Later he identified himself with narrower views, and on the utbreak of the Russian Revolution he was appointed Bolshevik Consul or Glasgow.

t the General Election in 1918, following the Armistice, he stood as a ocialist candidate for the Gorbals Division of Glasgow against Mister ieorge N. Barnes, then a member of the Government. He had intended come forward as a Republican for the division on this occasion and ad addressed several meetings, his last being on Sunday evening. ome surprise was occasioned when he failed to attend for nomination, nd later it was learned he had become unwell.

n the last year or two he contested several of the municipal wards of ıe city, and among his other activities he took a prominent part in ounding a Labour College in Glasgow for which he was a lecturer in conomics." *[Breaks off and looks up.]* What do you think?

DITOR: *[Stifles yawn.]* There's still a bit of rubbish can be cut out if ve need the space. And say something a bit more detrimental about ilasgow. It's something the boss likes to see. I'll leave it to you.

UB: *[Scribbling.]* That should be straightforward enough.

DITOR: *[In a confiding manner.]* At dinner tonight I heard something was quite pleased about.

UB: To do with the paper?

EDITOR: No. About me. It was just a hint. I might be on the next Honours List.

SUB: *[Standing.]* Congratulations! How sure are you?

EDITOR: One of the Unionists whispered it to me. Told me not to say anything but it's usually definite when it reaches this stage. *[Obviously pleased with himself.]*

SUB: A small celebration in advance? *[Rises and fetches a bottle and two glasses from a cupboard. He pours two large measures and they each hold a glass up in the manner of a toast.]* You deserve it for all the good work you have done over the years. Here's to you. Sir!

EDITOR: *[Smiling broadly.]* Cheers! *[They drink.]*

THE END

***

CAST

John Maclean
Agnes Maclean
George Watson
Refinery Workers
Jimmy MacDougall
Tom Kennedy
Police Officer
Peter Petroff
George Pollok
Robert Blair
Murdo MacDonald
Charles Diamond
Ian Fergusson
Ewan Campbell
Calum Innes
Chairman
H.M. Hyndman
Editor
Sub-editor
Lloyd George
Arthur Henderson
David Kirkwood
Prison Warder
Maintenance Engineers
Sir Auckland Geddes
Sir George Cave
Winston Churchill
Ruaraidh Erskine
Theodore Rothstein
Lieutenant Colonel Malone, M.P.
Inkpin
Cant
Lord Curzon
Permanent Secretary

Crofters
Sheriff Boyd
Rev William Fulton
Mrs Shevlin

The play has been written with the intention of needing the minimum of characters and props.

***